Wado-Ryu Karate Uncovered

by

Frank Johnson

www.orient-publishing.com

ISBN 1-873861-03-6

DISCLAIMER

The publishers of this book WILL NOT BE HELD RESPONSIBLE in any way whatsoever for any physical injury, or damage of any sort, that may occur as a result of reading and/or following the instructions given herein. It is essential therefore, that before attempting any of the physcial activites described or depicted in this book, the reader or readers should consult a qualified physician to ascertain whether the reader or readers should engage in the physical activity described or depicted in this book.

As the physcial activities described or depicted herein may be overly taxing or sophisticated for the reader or readers, it is *essential that this advice be followed and a physician consulted.*

Book cover by Alec Hawkins

Designed and typeset in 11/13 Sabon by Welshpool Printing Group, Severn Farm Enterprise Park, Welshpool, Powys, SY21 7DF, UK.

Contents

Frank scoring with a Mawashigeri (Roundhouse kick) - All Japan 1978.

Foreword

It is every Karate student's dream who has reached any reasonable standard, to travel to the birth place of many of today's martial arts in Japan. For many, the cost and time off from work and their family ties etc., this is a far off reality.

As I have travelled around the country countless people have asked me what it is like to train in Japan, or if I would go to their club and give a talk on training in Japan; I have always declined their offer. To me, Karate training has always been a personal thing, and being a little shy with people I don't know makes it difficult for me to talk about my own training. It was with this in mind and the constant barrage of questions on the subject that I agreed to put down on paper some of the memories of my time in Japan. I have tried to write the book in a way that reflects what I was thinking at the time and have put in stories that looking back now are quite amusing, but at the time were deadly serious.

For those that are contemplating going to Japan I would give you this piece of advice: Put all your heart into your training and never give up, even when it seems impossible. Have a go and you will surely benefit from your experiences in Japan.

Acknowledgement

I am indebted to countless people for their help with this book, and those whom I have trained with over the years. Especially my Mother and Father for all their help and support over the years; to my wife Christine, and to Sensei Sakagami for all his help over the years. To my other Japanese Instructors in England Master Tatsuo Suzuki. To my Instructors in Japan Grand Master Hironori Ohtsuka, Master Thoru Arakawa, Master Inoue Motokatsu, Sensei Hisao Murase and Sensei Meada.

Frank with Hisao Murase - All Japan Champion

Preparing to go to Japan

It was in 1976 I first seriously thought about travelling to Japan to further my study of martial arts and in particular Wado-Ryu Karate.

I had just passed my first Dan and was feeling like I could take on the whole Japanese national team on my own; anyone who has passed their black belt will know what I mean. I began by reading all the books I could find on Japan as well as sending for one of those learn at home language courses you often see advertised in the newspapers and set about trying to learn Japanese. By the spring of 1977 I had mastered a few words but I found it very difficult, it turned out that it is not really that important for a Karate student to know. Most Japanese Instructors have made an effort to learn some English and after a while you start to pick up the language and can usually get by.

For some time I had been travelling to Wolverhampton from my home on the English/Welsh border to be trained by Sensei Kuniaki Sakagami 7th Dan, one of the best Instructors in Wado-Ryu outside Japan. The distance from my home was some 92 miles round trip. Petrol at that time was only around sixty pence a gallon which was not too bad, though it took longer to get there and back than I spent on training at the Club. When I was there I realised that I needed much more instruction if I was to improve.

I asked Sensei Peter May, the Senior English black belt at Wolverhampton what he thought of my problem. After some discussion, training in Japan came up. I asked Sensei May if he thought Sensei Sakagami would give me a letter of Introduction and he advised me to ask him. So a few weeks later, when the opportunity arose, with some nervousness, I told him of my wish to go to Japan and could he advise me on my best course of action. Sensei Sakagami was very helpful, he told me what I was likely to find, how very expensive Japan was and that June and July was not a good time to go as the humidity in Tokyo was very high around then. He advised me to go to the Tokyo Physical Centre, the Headquarters of Wado-Ryu at that time in Japan in Tokyo. It turned out to be the greatest Karate Club I have ever trained in. Sensei Sakagami also said that he would write me a letter of introduction, to which I am eternally grateful.

So, with all this information I sent a letter to the Japanese Embassy in London and asked for a visa to study Karate. A few weeks later I received a reply saying that I may stay in Japan for up to six months and that if I wished to stay longer I must apply in Japan. I made up my mind to go in the September of 1977 and try to stay the six months; as it happens it was to be nearly two years before I was to return home. I should point out that at this stage in my life I had never been further from home than London for a week's Karate training at Crystal Palace, so the thought of flying to the other side of the world and not know anyone at the other end was a daunting prospect. With my parent's help I tried to plan for any problems that I might have to face. I placed all my money in a bank account that enabled me to telex some out if I needed it. Unfortunately, at the time the pound sterling was going through a bad patch and you were only allowed to take out of the country £300, which I was to discover is totally inadequate for someone arriving in Japan.

At last the big day arrived, my Mother and Father took me to the local railway station and I was on my way to Heathrow airport in London. My plane was due to take off at 10.30pm. After a little delay the plane took off and I looked down on the lights of London and wondered if I was doing the right thing. Sat next to me was a Japanese Doctor, he told me that he had come to England to play golf. I was to find out later that joining a golf club in Japan was almost as costly as buying one in England!

The plane stopped at Abu Dhabu to re-fuel, after which we went on to Karachi, Bangkok, Thailand and at last Tokyo. By this time I had been awake for 36 hours and I had, for a better word, jet lag. The door of the plane opened and for a second it seemed like I was back home, it was raining cats and dogs, and the raindrops were bouncing off the tarmac runway about two inches. I ran to the waiting bus and was ushered into the customs hall.

My first day in Japan

"Why have you come to Japan?" the custom man said. "To do Karate", I replied. "You're very young to travel on your own, do you have a return ticket?" he asked. I showed him my ticket. "How long will you be staying?" "I hope about six months". "That's a long time, where will you be going?" I told him, with that he seemed to be happy and assured that I knew what I was doing, and with the words "enjoy your stay" I passed into the main arrival area and Tokyo's Handa Airport. By this time I was feeling quite ill from the air flight; I decided I needed some good English food, I went to the airport restaurant and had the nearest thing to home cooking I could buy, which turned out to be hamburger and French fries.

Feeling a little better I then had the problem of finding somewhere to stay the night. I went to the information desk and explained to them that I didn't want a very expensive hotel. They suggested the Y.M.C.A. at £15 a night which was cheap as hotels went in Tokyo. Armed with the address I found a taxi, gave him the address and was on my way into Tokyo itself.

The first thing I noticed was that they drive on the same side of the road as in Britain. The volume of traffic in Central Tokyo was rather heavy. The sky over the centre looked rather dirty from car fumes and low level clouds. Everyone looked very busy and well dressed, the men in suits and the ladies in smart dresses. By the time I had reached the hotel the fare for the taxi was around £25 – the words of Sensei Sakagami, that it was expensive in Japan, were ringing in my ears. I had only been in Japan about two hours and had already spent around £40 of my £300 but I was too tired to worry about that. I booked into the hotel and was shown my room. I sat on the bed and turned on the television, I started to get ready for bed when the bed started to shake, and the television started to shake off its stand. It was an earthquake, something that happens all the time in Japan; but quite a shock to an English man who has never experienced such an event. At last I settled down and as soon as my head touched the pillow I fell fast asleep.

Frank outside Wado-Ryu headquarters.

Arriving at the headquarters of Wado-Ryu

The next day I awoke late and proceeded to the toilet, to my surprise there was not one, in any case not an English style one. Japanese toilets are built flat on the floor. After discovering how it worked I went down to breakfast. This was my first Japanese meal. I had a bowl of rice, some soup that reminded me of Oliver Twist in the work-house, some pickles and green tea. I was so hungry that I ate the lot with gusto and it did not taste too bad at all.

My problem now was how to get to the Karate club. The man on the desk at the hotel could speak some English, so I asked him the best way to get there. He told me to get the underground to Shibuya station and then a taxi. I took his advice. Luckily for a foreigner in Tokyo the station names are in English as well as Japanese, so without too much trouble I got to Shibuya and then found a taxi, I gave him the address of the club and we were soon there. It was late afternoon by the time I had arrived at the club, after paying the taxi driver I looked for a way in. There was a big sign saying "Tokyo Physical Centre", the club was below street level, above it was a restaurant. The door of the club was open but no-one was there. I decided to go to the restaurant to ask where someone was. I was shown up to the first floor of the building and pointed out a door. I straightened my tie and knocked on the door, it was opened by a powerfully built man of around 5 feet 10 inches tall. I immediately recognised him as a Hisao Murase, three times champion of Japan. I had seen him earlier that year when the Japanese University team had taken on the United Kingdom Karate – Do Wado Kai, he had destroyed all before him including Jeff Thompson (who went on to win many world championships). With a fantastic foot sweep reverse punch combination, that sticks in my mind to this day. He asked me into the office to be greeted by a Mr. T. Meada, who later went on to win the 65 kgs world title in Spain in 1980. A very brave little man with a great fighting spirit and a lethal front kick – as I was to find out later to my cost.

They sat me down and asked me where I had come from. They seemed genuinely pleased that I had come so far to train at their club. I gave Sensei Murase the letter Mr. Sakagami had given me, Murase said he would give it to the Chief Instructor Master Thoru Arakawa 7th Dan, he would be coming back to the office soon.

The office was a hive of activity, I was told it was where most of the work was done in organising Wado-Ryu in Japan. At that time it was in full swing sorting out the 4th world Karate championships coming up in Tokyo in about twelve weeks time. After a little while Master Arakawa arrived and sat down to read the letter, after some time, which seemed to me like a lifetime, he looked up and with a big smile said that I may stay at the club as long as I wished. He asked me if I had somewhere to stay, "Not yet" I replied. He asked one of the secretaries to find a cheap hotel near the club. After taking me there he announced that training would start at 5 p.m. the next day and that a student would come to pick me up so that I would not get lost on my first day. By this time I was feeling a lot better in myself and my jet lag was beginning to wear off. The hotel was a Japanese style one and cost around £12 a night. I was shown to my room, it had a small table and the bed was on the floor.

After a little while, the landlady knocked on the door and showed me the bathroom, I thanked her in the little bit of Japanese I knew and proceeded to have a bath. After my bath I pulled out the plug which proved to be a big mistake. Some while later there was a knock at the door, I opened it to find a distraught landlady beckoning me to the bathroom and pointing to the bath, I looked at it thinking I must not have cleaned it out properly or something; I really could not understand what all the fuss was about and went back to my room.

The next day, around 4 p.m. one of the students came down to take me to the club. After talking to the landlady he told me, in broken English, that when you go for a bath in Japan you wash outside the bath and just use the bath to soak in, you do not pull the plug out as other people want to use it.

When he told me this I could see why she was not too happy, I asked him to say I was sorry and that it would not happen again. She smiled like mothers do to their sons, I picked up my Karate suit and was on my way to my first lesson in Japan.

"I told you your defence was no good", Frank, san.

Karate Ni Sentenashi - is very important in karate training. The Karateka must never attack first physically or mentally, years of hard correct training are needed, as the Karateka becomes better he also grows in good manners, etiquette, outwardly and even more important inwardly.

My first lesson in Japan

I arrived at the club at about 4.30 in the afternoon. After changing into my suit I went into a corner to warm up on my own. By the time the class was due to start some fifteen black belts and around the same number of brown and white belts had arrived. The club was not that large, so when you have thirty or so it started to get a bit cramped. Along one side of the club there was a big mirror, some wall mounted Makiwaras (punching boards), a big punch bag and weights of different kinds. There was also a small changing room, a sauna and shower room; in fact a very nice compact club. Most of the students were ex-students of different universities or students that had come from other clubs for the high standard of instruction that the club offered. As well as their own members quite a lot of non-Japanese passed through the club, but most of them didn't stop for more than a few lessons during the time I was there.

After a little while Murase Sensei and Maeda Sensei came in and we all lined up for the bows. We then had about twenty minutes of exercises, we did sit-ups, each student counting out ten, followed by press-ups and more exercises for your stomach – fifty leg rises, this involved lying on your back grabbing your partner's legs and lifting your legs up until they touched your partner's body. By this time I was already beginning to sweat as it was still quite warm in September. We lined up and began basic techniques including hundreds of front kicks and step forward snap punches to the face. This punch called Tobikomizuki in Wado-Ryu improved so much during my time in Japan that I have never failed to hit the target when I have had to save myself from harm, and have derived a great deal of satisfaction from this punch over the years. For that I must thank Murase for making me do so many.

After a short rest to get our breath back, there was a shout of command from Murase and we were off on a run through the streets of Tokyo, we always ran bare foot unless you had a good excuse to wear some Zori (slippers). Fortunately, the streets are very clean and I never had any bad cuts on these runs. After ten minutes or so we arrived at the local shrine where there were some twenty steps up to the top. "Get someone on your back and run up the steps", came the order. I seemed to get the biggest student and being only five feet four and eight and a half stone at the time I found this almost impossible; but somehow I did it and after doing it twice I was completely exhausted. We lined up bowed to the shrine and ran back shouting loud Kiais as we went to keep up our spirits.

When we arrived back at the club Sensei Arakawa was getting changed. After a little rest to get our breath back and to wash our feet, we lined up to do our bows, the senpai (senior) going first followed by the kohai (junior), we all bowed to Arakawa Sensei then paired off to practice Kihon Gumite (these techniques are a series of attacks and defences, using traditional moves of martial arts and developed by the founder of Wado-Ryu professor Hironori Ohtsuka). Arakawa told me that Kihon Gumite was offensive as well as defensive, a nice phrase which has stuck with me to this day. We then did some fighting moves, all the students were then told to sit down for Ji-yu-kumite (free sparring). I was called up to do my thing for King and Country. No sooner had Arakawa said Hajami (start) then I got hit on the nose and it started to bleed, followed by one in the eye and a kick in the groin. I started to back pedal out of harms way, this was followed by Arakawa shouting, "don't go back, don't go back", and kicking me up the backside. After about five minutes of this the night's training began to tell and my legs would not move off the spot and felt like lead. Mercifully, a halt was called and I walked back to the side of the dojo (training hall), Arakawa still shouting at me not to go back so much in the future, my pride was shot to pieces, after a while the class came to an end.

The class had lasted over four hours and I was completely exhausted, but somehow I felt good that I had lasted till the end. Arakawa asked if I would like to go and help the club by supporting them in a competition that was to be held tomorrow. Thanking him I walked back to my hotel stopping off at a small restaurant for some food. I arrived back at my hotel, had a bath making sure I did not pull the plug out this time and settled down to sleep. I promised myself I wouldn't go back so much next time.

I awoke the next morning to find that I could hardly get out of bed. I was so stiff, and was happy that there was going to be no training that day. I had my breakfast and went up to the club to meet the lads. Most of the students had a good laugh about my black eye from the night before which was nearly closed, but the laughter was in no way vindictive and I can honestly say I got on well with everyone in the club when I got to know them.

The competition was to be held in a local school sports hall. The first thing I noticed was the lack of kicking, nine out of ten techniques were punches and the only kick employed really was maegeri (front kick). I don't recall seeing Mawashigeri (round house kicks), used a lot in European competitions. In the whole contest this did surprise me a little, there was no doubt that punching was much sharper over all than back home, the control was good, in any case it was in this tournament.

During a break in the tournament I was asked to go with some of the lads to buy some bentos (Japanese lunch boxes) for the club members to eat. These bentos have lots of different compartments of food such as rice, sweets and sushi and are eaten cold, almost like the ready dinners you can buy back home. I was given the job of asking for them. After almost giving the shop keeper a heart attack I blurted out the word bento and a relieved shop keeper put them in a bag for me. I soon got used to getting things from shops, if I did not know the word for it I would point at it and say, "give me that" they always got the message.

The tournament was won by Murase, but not easily, he had one or two hard fights and received a nice black eye, proving that getting a black eye in Japan was as common as having a cup of tea back home for students and champions alike.

Over the next few months I worked hard to overcome my problem of going back too much when doing ji-yu-kumite (free sparring) this was difficult. Nevertheless I had to over come it if I was going to make progress in traditional Karate. This was what I had come to Japan for rather than learning how to be a better contest fighter.

The T.P.C. club was not that big so you could not move around like many contest fighters, or keep going back a little at a time hoping to hit him as he came in. There was no such thing as hanging around, the fighting was non stop all out war. If a student was unlucky enough to find himself up against the wall he would have to fight his way out. It was not uncommon for a student to get his head pushed into the wall if he was not careful to get away. An American, named John found himself up against a wall one evening when he was free sparring Murase sensei, John stopped and dropped his guard just as Murase let go of a Mawashi-geri (round house kick) hitting him in the jaw breaking it in two places, which resulted in him losing two stone in weight as he could only drink liquids for seven weeks while his jaw was wired up. Fortunately I never had such a bad injury.

This kind of free sparring demands lots of guts and determination and fitness and is certainly not for the weak hearted. Guts and determination is a very important part of traditional Karate, and to keep fighting whenever you're getting a beating off your better is all part of forming your spirit, rather than thinking he is a sadist for picking on you. You should train harder to overcome the weakness he has shown you.

One of the problems I encountered was the time free sparring actually lasted anything from five to twenty minutes non-stop, at full speed and usually against one person. This I found at the start quite hard. When the club was preparing for a tournament the sparring was much longer. After a while I began to really enjoy this kind of sparring and still think it is the best way to do free sparring. Though hard for beginners it does build your character it gives you time to beat your partner mentally as well as physically. As the fight goes on you have to dig deep into your physical powers but even more important you have to dig deep into your mental powers to keep going especially if you are fighting someone better than yourself.

Lots of Karate-ka in Europe have very bad habits, especially those that are only interested in contest fighting, such as leaving their legs too wide apart making it easy to kick the groin or their fingers open and pointing forward. An American visiting the club one evening had two of his fingers broken when one of the students accidentally punched him on the hand. While points like these may not help you win a contest they can lose you the real fight very quickly. Many Europeans stop after each point or move and if they hit their opponent by accident they stop and say sorry and momentarily relax, giving time to their adversary to get over the first successful move. I don't think I heard the word "Sorry" in free sparring ever in Japan, if you are a genuine person who fights hard but does not go out deliberately to hurt your opponent then there is no need to use the word "Sorry" in the dojo.

Another habit that is very important to get out of and from my experience can not be over emphasised, is when you are hit in the face or body; no matter how good you are, some time you will receive a blow that hurts a little at first. When I was hit I just stopped fighting, thinking about the pain of it, especially if I was hit in the face, but my opponent just kept hitting me if I did stop. At first I thought I was getting special treatment, but I soon realised that stopping when I had not been knocked down was the way to certain defeat. You must keep going and fighting back at all costs. If you're hit on the nose it may make your eyes water but you must keep fighting back. If you are hit hard and your ears are buzzing, you must keep going. "If you are hit, immediately attack back as hard as you can" was the motto of the club and I soon learnt it was a good one.

Frank's small flat in Tokyo.

19

SU   - indicates that a beginner must correctly copy all karate techniques from his instructor.

HA - means that after a number of years of training, when the karateka has attained a high degree back belt, he is allowed to develop new techniques provided they are improvements. This applies to all movements with the exception of basic techniques.

RI   - is the highest form. It means that after an even longer period of training than for HA, the Karateka must be able to perform all forms of karate automatically.

Working in Japan

As the weeks past I realised that if I was going to stay in Japan I would have to find some kind of job. Soon after training one evening I went to have a meal in the restaurant above the club. The chef was always very kind to the karate students and used to keep us any food that was left over, as we were always very hungry after training. John, the American that later had his jaw broken, could speak Japenese quite well as he had been going in and out of Japan for a number of years. This particular evening, the Chef mentioned to John that the restaurant up the road was looking for a washer-up to help out in the day; it would not be much money but I could eat as much as I wanted if I wished. The Chef offered to take me up to see the owner the next day and explain my position.

Next morning I went to see the owner, a Mr Tadatsura Ogawa. I did not know at the time that it was one of the best French restaurants in Tokyo. He seemed to think it would be good to have a foreigner working at the restaurant for a while, I was to start the next day at 9 a.m., and finish at 4 p.m., that, he said would give me an hour to rest before my training starts at 5 p.m. I would be paid at the end of each month and get three meals a day. Food and plenty of it is what I needed as I used up a lot of calories in training each day. Thanking Mr Ogawa for his kindness I started work next morning. I shall always remember the kindness shown to me at Ogawaken and especially a man named Watanabe, he was told to see that I did everything right and was a good friend all through my time in Japan. When I arrived in the morning my first job was making the consume, this involved chopping up bones and meat and such like and boiling them up in a big cauldron. Each morning a big plastic bucket of frogs were delivered for frog legs. These frogs resulted in a lot of laughter when one day, as a joke, I was asked to kill them. I hovered over the frog trying to put an end to it with a big knife, they just could not understand how a black belt in Karate and training at the famous Wado-Ryu dojo down the road, did not have the nerve to kill a frog. It was one of many laughs I had at Ogawaken.

The restaurant opened from 11.30 a.m. to 2 p.m. in the day. This was always a busy time, I was the chief washer up and to this day it would not worry me if I never put a cloth to a dish ever again. The dishes were never ending. Doing all this washing up was making my hands go soft and with doing makiwara training at the club they were getting quite a mess. Makiwara (padded post used to improve your punching) training at the club was not compulsory, but most of the black belts did do some. The type used were the wall mounted ones. These had a straw covering and springs that help take the shock of the punch and came out from the wall about eight inches or so. One day, one of the white belts missed the makiwara and, over stretching, hit the wall at the back resulting in his knuckle being smashed back into his hand. After this accident the makiwara was taken down off the wall while it was decided what action was going to be taken. There really was no room inside the club for a floor mounted one.

I welcomed the time for my hands to heal from all the washing up and, to this day I feel that this type of wall-mounted makiwara should be avoided by beginners as they just do not have the control and accuracy and risk injury. After around four months at Ogawaken I found a job teaching English that only involved working two days a week. This gave me much more time to practice. It was sad to leave the friends at the restaurant but they understood that I had only come to Japan to improve my knowledge of martial arts and time was very important to me.

The World Karate Championships

I had been in Japan about eight weeks when teams began arriving for the fourth world championships which was to be held at the Nippon Budokan, the main martial arts hall in Tokyo on the 3rd and 4th December 1977. The T.P.C. club was to be used by many of the countries taking part and I had an interesting time watching the different approaches to their training. One of the teams at the club was Iran, which did well in the tournament, coming joint third with France. In Iran's team was a massive man named Salimi, weighing in at 16 stone and 6 feet 8 inches tall, he became quite a celebrity in the championships. Every time he attacked, he would shout out "Al, Lah", if he won he shouted out "Al, Lah be praised", and on one occasion he ran around the outside of the fighting area with his fist closed and raised above his head shouting "Al Lah be praised, Al Lah be praised" to the annoyance of the officials and the cheers of the crowd.

The British team were staying at the New Otani hotel, the same hotel used in the James Bond Movie 'You Only Live Twice'. The team manager was Alex McGregor and coach Roy Stanhope. I went to the hotel to meet Roy and spend the day with the team. As I arrived the party was just returning from their morning training run and a game of football against a local team that happened to be practising near the hotel. The British team won three one, I was told, but I don't know if a bit of Karate was used to get the result. Anyway it was a nice break for the team. After breakfast we went to the American club in Tokyo to train. It had a good sports hall, I was particularly impressed by Victor Charles who looked very sharp and powerful and David Donavan looked good when attacking, in fact the team looked far better than any of the teams training at the T.P.C. club. The rest of the team were Tyrone White, Alec Duncan, Peter Dennis,

Stanley Knighton, Eugene Codrington, David Colter, Royston Jerime and Oswald Rowe. I wished them luck and went back to the T.P.C. club for my own training.

It was around the time of the championships that I moved into a small flat. When I say flat it cannot be compared to a flat in England. It was just one room. Any kind of accommodation in Tokyo is very expensive as so many people live and work there. I paid 10,000 yen a month, that was around £50 at the time. It was a little way from the club at a place called Oyama, this being a bit outside the main City helped make it a lot cheaper. It was just a place to sleep and I spent very little time there, but it was nice to know that I had a place of my own to get away from the hustle and bustle of Tokyo.

As the day of the championships neared, Arakawa sensei asked me if I would go along early on the morning of the championships to help out if needed. I arrived at 7.00 a.m., it was an eerie feeling walking into an empty Budoken, but soon the place was a hive of activity as officials and teams began to arrive. The tournament was opened at 10.00 a.m. by Mr. F. Takagi, chairman of the organising committee. The first event was to be men's Kata (series of techniques performed alone) this was the first time it had been included in the world championships. At this time there was no ladies Kata or Kumite (contest sparring) but plans were under way to include ladies at the next championships to be held in Madrid, Spain in two years time. There was a lot of controversy over this event when the judges changed the rules in mid contest from any Kata to only selected ones, which meant that some of the contestants did not know any of the selected Katas. One contestant accused the Japanese of gross bias towards their own contestants. I don't know if that was true or not, but it was won by Kenji Okado of Japan doing Seipai. After the controversy of the kata, the team event got under way. The defending champions Great Britain's first match was against the Dominican Republic. Great Britain had an easy win and went into the second round where they met Japan.

Great Britain had never lost to Japan and Japan had never been defeated at home; you could feel the excitement as the two teams lined up. Great Britain's number one was Tyrone White and Japan's number one was my own Instructor, Murase sensei. Murase, who never got into the fight lost

24

by two Ippons (full points). After, Murase said it was not his day, a good way of looking at things, (his day was to come when he won the world open weight title in Taiwan in 1982). Next out was Eugene Codrington, which ended in a draw, Peter Dennis lost by one Ippon. Captain David Donovan also lost by one point. The last man out was Alec Duncan, what a job he had to pull Great Britain back.! He was put up against Junichiro Hamaguchi, who came second in the 1975 world championships. The contest was only about 30 seconds old when Alec hit him with a fantastic Mawashigeri that had Hamaguchi crawling around the floor stunned. I thought Duncan would be disqualified, as I could see from where I was sat that Hamaguchi was standing like a drunken man and did not know where he was. Instead they gave him Chui (warning). No sooner had the contest started again when Duncan scored with Gyakuzuki (reverse punch) four Ippons, the result was two wins each and one draw, but Great Britain had one win by two Ippons making Great Britain the winners and Japan's first loss in their own Country.

The second day got under way with the team quarter finals. Great Britain met West Germany. Everyone expected Britain to have an easy win; that was not to be the case, they lost by the same marginal score as their last against Japan. Germany went on to lose to the Netherlands in the final. So it was up to my two Countries Individuals to salvage something for the old Country. Tyrone White did well and went through the eliminating rounds, but lost to Juan Carvil of Spain in Encho-sen (extension). Meanwhile, Codrington was storming through to the final to meet Otti Roethof (Netherlands). Eugene was not on his best form in the final and lost by one Ippon scored with a good Gyakuzuki, so ended the 1977 world union of Karatedo organisations.

I can't let this section pass without saying something about the marvellous demonstrations that are really only possible in Japan. Lots of katas from top Masters, such as Suparimpei; this kata has 108 fighting techniques and said to contain many of the secrets of the Goju-Ryu style of Karate. Masters of all kinds of style did some kata or self defence demonstrations; the announcer taking a lot of great pleasure in saying that the masters present represented over 1000 years training in martial arts.

There was classical Japanese music and hundreds of children doing their basic punches and kicks, a nice gesture to make the children part of the day. To top it all W U K O president Sasakawa did a demonstration with Sumo, grand champion Jesse Takamiyama, throwing him all over the floor.

Black Belt training, Junzuki punch

Black Belt training, Junzuki-no-Tsukkomi

Sumo in Japan

In the last chapter I mentioned the great Sumo, Grand Champion Jesse Takamiyama the first Japanese to win the Emperors cup in Japan's great national sport, Sumo. Takamiyama weighed in at around 360 pounds and 6ft 4inches tall. He was like a living tank and a great favourite with the Japanese public. When he talked it came out like a growl as he had been hit in the throat which affected his speech. Such is the intensity of training for the Sumotori (a person that does Sumo) that he had no time to go into hospital for its correction. Sumotories training can be up to sixteen hours a day and harsh to the extreme, so much that not many Westerners would last a day. The Sumotori eat a large high calorie diet called "chanko-nabe", this is a kind of stew with vegetables, meat, chicken and bean curd made from soya beans. I tried to watch Sumo on T.V. whenever I could. Each year they have a number of tournaments called a Basho, lasting fifteen days. The sumotori has one contest each day and the one who wins the most contests in the top division, the Maku-uchi division, becomes Grand Champion.

Each day the basho is started by the lowest ranks and by the time T.V. coverage starts at around 6.00 p.m. the top men are in action. The idea is to push your adversary out of the dohyo first, or topple him over. The dohyo is an eighteen foot round mound of clay. The sumotori are not allowed to kick or punch during the contest. There is an elaborate pre-fight build-up, which includes throwing salt on the ground to purify the ring, stamping their feet and drinking (chikara-muzu) power water. Most fights last only a few seconds and are very exciting.

"Remember always to keep the correct stance" Frank san.

All Japan Championships

The All-Japan was to be held in the July of 1978 at the Nippon Budokan, the venue of the world championships some eight months earlier. The T.P.C. club was to enter a team and we had begun preparing for the event about a month before it was due.

The All-Japan is the highlight of the competition year and every club puts in a lot of extra training so as to be on top form that day. Two training sessions were set aside just for competition training. As the T.P.C. club was a private club it was not possible to have this kind of training every lesson.

As some of the students were not that young their days of competing in competition were passed, they had seen it all before, and done most of it, and although they encouraged us young ones they had lost interest in that side of karate which is understandable.

I would not describe myself as a great competition fighter but as a traditional Wado-Ryu exponent, so I was pleased to be asked to be part of the squad.

We would begin training by doing lots of stretching and strengthening exercises and a little bit of weight training. There is no great emphasis in Wado-Ryu on lifting heavy weights compared with some styles, for example in Goju-ryu karate they do a lot of weight training. After this we would make a large circle to practice kicking and punching. The top grade would begin by shouting out a technique, each student would count up to ten for every one doing the technique each time. If there were twenty or thirty there, that would mean doing the technique two or three hundred times. We nearly always started with step forward Tomikomizuki to the face, which was one of Murase's Sensei favourite techniques, followed by Maegri – front kick or Gyakuzuki – reverse punch, this kind of thing went on for about an hour, followed by combinations of kicking and punching up and down the room. By this time your suit would be wet through from the sweat of your efforts.

July is not a good time to train in Japan as the temperature and humidity would be about twenty celsius in Tokyo in afternoons and early evenings. We would have a short rest before running bare foot to the Konno Shrine, about a mile from the Club. When we returned we carried on with sparring techniques in pairs, finally some light competition sparring.

On the Monday, five days prior to the All-Japan I arrived at the club to find a four man team from England, which was quite a surprise, together with Sensei Tatsuo Suzuki, who asked me if I would make up the five man team for Saturday's All-Japan. In one way I was happy to represent my country, but a little disappointed that I would not be in the T.P.C. squad who I had been training with for so long, but my country came first, so I agreed.

We spent the afternoon training and Master Ohtsuka came down to see the lads, which was nice for them.

The team was made up of Geoff Thompson, who was to become one of the Great Britain squad members for the triple world championship victories in 1982, 1984 and 1986, together with Nieman Prince, who was a Great Britain team member and winner of the European Wado-Ryu championships, Unel Wellington from Wales and Kata Exponent Kevin Jones who had unfortunately lost a hand in an accident some years earlier and had a leather capping on the stump, to be hit by this was something never to be forgotten!

After training we had a long talk about what was happening at home. The lads were going to spend the next few days getting acclimatized to Japan. I had a few more training sessions before I wound down my training. I wished them a good time and promised to meet them at the Budoken at 8 a.m. on Saturday morning.

The next evening an American team arrived at the Club to compete in the Championships. They asked Arakawa Sensei if they could train with the T.P.C. class that evening. All the American men were big, we had a hard lesson, no doubt due to the Americans being there and the heat and humidity took its toll on everyone, especially the Americans. During a rest period some of the Americans asked if they could free spar with the black belts from the Club. I thought they are either very good or crazy, it was to be the latter. They took a fearful beating, one of them commented that it was Pearl Harbour all over again! I did my best to assure them that I went through the same thing, but it was not much help to people with black eyes and bleeding noses. Their coach said "Don't worry lads, it must be the jet-lag".

The 1978 All Japan was to see some one hundred and thirty teams, split into two groups, private clubs and university teams and about two hundred in the individual event. Everyone competing was black belt standard.

Universities are the main source of the top competition fighters in Japan. Most students spend four years at a University karate club, training about four hours each day. Before Championships and special courses they would train all day and every day. They usually enter University at eighteen or nineteen years of age, staying until they reach the age of twenty-one or twenty-two. Their training has to fit in with their studies, which can be a little tiring, but they manage somehow. Many of the karate students study for a degree in Economics, which seems to be the favourite subject for would be Masters of the Martial Arts. A good education is a must if you want to get on in the very competitive society in Japan and when your University days are over if you are not fortunate enough to find a job teaching karate or find a sponsor you will need your degree to fall back on.

The top University over the years for Wado-Ryu had been Nichi-Dai, this club has produced some of the world's top Masters, such as Sensei Fuji and Masafumi Shiomitsu to name but a couple.

The Championships were due to start at 9 a.m. Dead on time the teams lined up, after a few opening speeches a big drum was struck signalling the start of the tournament, the drum is struck slowly at first, continuing to get faster, finishing in a crescendo of noise, sending an air of excitement throughout the arena. Our first contest was against a team from Tokyo, I was placed in fifth fighting position. Geoff Nieman and Unel all won, Kevin drew, we were therefore through to the next round so I was not under pressure to win but I was still nervous as I went out for this, my first fight of the day. No sooner had I started the fight I hit my opponent as he was coming in in the face, it was no way intentional on my part, but it knocked him right over, thinking this would get me disqualified, and in Europe it would have done. But the All-Japan at that time it seems was one of those tournaments where you only get disqualified if you put your opponent into hospital, so all that was said was "Be careful next time". The fight ended in a draw and we went into the next round.

Meanwhile the American team was doing its best and had one or two good wins before finally losing in the second round. Our second round match was against a team from the outskirts of Tokyo, once again when it came to my turn to fight I had to draw or win for us to stay in the competition, I attacked him from the beginning with mawashigeri (roundhouse kick to the head) scoring quite easily as his guard was very low, this must have upset him a little because he attacked me fiercely hitting me high upon the forehead with a punch, the force of the blow knocked me back and out of the square fighting area, and made a small round mark where the spin of his fist had taken the skin off. I staggered back into the square knowing that my opponent was only going to get a warning. I scored on him immediately the fight restarted, a few seconds later the bell sounded for the end of the fight, putting us into the next round. We were to have thirty minutes rest before we were due to fight a powerful team from Osaka. Included in the Osaka team was a fourth Dan named Masade who had the reputation of being a hard nut. He was an unusual fighter as he kept his head very low and his body crouched, he reminded me a little of the former world heavy weight boxing champion, Joe Frasier. He spent most of his time kicking to the groin, coming up from his low stance he would do forward lightning attacks, a real handful in anyone's book.

We had a good start to the match thanks to Nieman and Geoff. Unel was to fight Masade, Unel was under heavy pressure from the beginning as

Masade was trying to head butt him and kick him in the groin, as Unel was over six feet tall, and Masade was fighting with his head low and body crouched, Unel had to punch down into him all the time. During one of Masade's lightning forward attacks Unel hit him full force on top of his head. Masade shook his head just like a bull, the referee called an end to the bout and it was a draw. Unel sat down and took off his fighting mitt, his hand was visibly getting bigger, it was obvious he had broken it on Masade's head in the last few seconds of the bout.

Next out was Kevin Jones who unfortunately just lost by a narrow margin leaving it that I had to draw or win, things went my way and I won by half a point. We were now through to the last sixteen. It was unfortunate that we were now drawn against my own Club, the T.P.C. which included three of Japan's National team. Nieman faced Murase in a very exciting contest in which he tried to take down Murase with a scissors technique but just failed to succeed. Murase scored shortly after this to take the bout. Geoff won his bout making it one all. The next fight was Unel who's hand by this time had swollen up to twice its size, so much in fact that he couldn't get his mitt on. He was to fight Maeda, who he had fought in England some twelve months previous, beating him, so Maeda was out to settle the score. From the beginning Maeda attacked Unel furiously and as much as Unel tried he was powerless to do much with a broken hand, he managed to hang on to a draw. Kevin under tremendous pressure was forced out of the fighting area and half a point was awarded against him, therefore I had to win to stay in the Championships. By sheer fate I faced my old adversary, Jaws with whom I had already had a bust up with some months previous, by this time he had acquired his black belt. He scored first after a few seconds, I scored in reply with my favourite punch, step forward Tomikomizuki to the face, but a draw was no use, and time was fast running out. I attacked furiously but to no avail. I just could not get another score on him, so at the final bell the referee gave a draw. We had lost by half a point to my own Club. The T.P.C. club went on to reach the final, they were beaten by Nich-Dai Old Boys, coached by the legendary Fuji.

After the championships we were invited to a very nice reception at one of the top hotels in Tokyo. All the top Instructors were there including Master Ohtsuka who sang an old martial arts song for us. After wishing the lads a good trip home I went back to my flat, tired but happy that we had put up a good performance. I awoke the next day black and blue especially my legs, which appeared to be purple instead of white. After breakfast I hobbled off to the club to see if I could train off some of the stiffness from the previous day. I arrived at the Club to find most of the T.P.C. team were celebrating their victory over the English opposition, so ended the weekend of my first All Japanese Championships.

After a hard days training Karate suits are hung up to dry.

Visa's, immigration and Korea

One of the problems most martial arts students coming to Japan encounter is how long the immigration Authorities will allow you to stay in the Country. This can become a real nightmare if you are not careful. Japan is one of the hardest Countries to get a visa.

My passport had been stamped for sixty days on entry at Haneda airport, I was told I could stay longer if I asked for an extension. After I had been in Japan for around fifty days, I went along to the local council offices and explained my position and that I wished to stay much longer than sixty days. They immediately gave me an extension for another sixty days and a small green book which I was to carry with me in case any police or immigration officials stopped me and wanted to know if I was entitled to be there. I was advised that my best course of action to stay longer would be to apply for a students visa, for which I would need to apply for outside Japan; this is not as complicated as it sounds. Korea is only an hour from Japan by plane and a new visa can be applied for there without too much trouble, so long as all your papers are in order. I would need a letter from someone in Japan to verify that I was of good character. Many of my fellow students at the club very kindly offered to give me one. So, with all my papers in order I went to book a flight to Seoul, Korea at the International students office in Tokyo where flights are cheaper for students. I had a choice of flying from Tokyo or Osaka, Japan's second largest City, some 300 miles from Tokyo. I chose Osaka, as it would give me a chance to see a little of that part of Japan, and it was also half the cost. The quickest way to Osaka was by the world famous Shinkansen (bullet trains) but they are expensive and travelling at 120 miles per hour I wouldn't see very much, so I decided to hitch hike. Not many people hitch hike in Japan, when I told my friend, Watanabe of my plans he thought I was mad, but agreed to write a sign for me saying, "English Student Wishes To Go To Osaka".

It is illegal to go on the Expressway on foot in Japan, so two days before my plane was due to leave I rose early and went by underground to the nearest road to the Expressway with my sign. No sooner had I lifted it up, a businessman who was on his way to Yokohoma, stopped and gave me a lift (Yokohoma is the main port of Japan and is heavily industrialised). When I was dropped off I was some fifty miles from Tokyo. I soon got another lift from a lorry driver who was going all the way to Osaka. As we moved away from Tokyo the countryside began to get very mountainous. We passed Mount Fuji, the top covered in snow which on a clear day could be seen from the skyscrapers in Tokyo. The expressway followed the coast for around two hundred miles as far as Nagoya, Japan's third largest City. Then we headed for Kyoto, the former home of the Imperial Palace. Along the route the road carved through mountains that resulted in long tunnels that never seemed to end. At last after twelve hours of travel the lights of Osaka could be seen in the darkening sky. The lorry driver dropped me off near the Y.M.C.A. where I was going to stay; I was glad of a bath and a good nights sleep.

The next day I went to see the famous Osaka castle, this castle was the stronghold of Hidyoshi, one of the last rivals to the first shogun (military ruler) of Japan, Tokugawa Ieyasus. The castle was stormed in 1616 after a long siege all the last occupants committed suicide. Parts of the castle were bombed in the second world war (like most big Cities Osaka has a population of around three million) it was very nearly flattened by United States bombers dropping ten's of thousands of tonnes of bombs towards the end of the second world war; but these days no signs can be found of those dark days less than forty years ago.

The following day I boarded a Korean airline plane and was on the short haul to Seoul. The only memory of the flight was a cup of Ginseng tea I had that tasted of dirty water and undrinkable to me.

The following day I went to the Japanese Embassy in Seoul and handed in my passport and papers, I was told to come back the next day to pick it up. When I picked it up I discovered it was stamped for another six months which could be extended without having to leave Japan. Feeling happy that I had sorted that problem out I had two days to look around before flying back to Japan. I asked at the hotel if they had any idea where a club was that practised the Korean martial art of Taekwondo. I was given an address and got a taxi driver to take me there.

I arrived as the club was practising Kata, or "forms" as they like to call them. They reminded me a little of Shotokan Karate. Then they did some free sparring, using around 70% leg movements, it seemed that more use was made of the body turning, rather than the hips to get the power as you do in Karate when kicking. I thanked the instructors the best I could for their hospitality, but they would not let me go and insisted that I went with them for a drink and something to eat. I was taken to a small restaurant with dead snakes hanging from hooks on the ceiling. One of the Instructors, seeing me looking at them said, "You like? You like"? and promptly ordered a yellow one to be brought down for inspection. Snake is apparently a delicacy in Korea. A piece of it was chopped off and cooked on the spot, to the delight of my host and to my horror! I did my best to eat as much as possible, it tasted like an English kipper to me. I enjoyed the company of my hosts and it was obvious to me that even though they did a completely different art, they were genuine martial artists and good people. It would be a long time before I would forget my snake meal with my Taekwondo friends.

Another kind of martial art practiced in Korea, but not so well known in the west, is Ssirum, traditional Korean wrestling, which is a little like Japanese Sumo. This is practiced at shows and fetes.

On my last day in Korea I decided to have a good look around the shops and streets to get a feel of the life style. People were well wrapped up, as Seoul is quite cold in December. On the corners of streets men would be selling sweet hot potatoes, nuts and small cakes. There were small shows of jugglers or strong men. One man tied piano wire around his body then asked one of the watching crowd to tighten it up with a pair of pliers, then with a great shout flexed his muscles and broke the wire to the cheers of the crowd. There were many signs saying no photographs, the military were still, it seems, very worried about spies after the Korean War some thirty years ago.

The next day it almost seemed as if I was going home when I boarded the plane on my way back to Japan – happy that the visas for my stay were sorted out and that trip would not be necessary again.

Unusual snow in Tokyo from the window of my small room.

New Year in Japan

Japan's main holiday is New Year and around this time of year many martial art clubs do demonstrations. The T.P.C. club was to do one the day before the break of training for New Year. I was asked as the foreigner in the club to do a Kata as part of the demonstration. Many of the top masters were there making it a bit of a nerve-wracking experience for a first Dan (degree). I was asked to do Ku-Shanku, this is one of the longest in the Wado-Ryu style and one of the oldest that is recorded. It has been passed down that a man named Koshokun came to Okinawa in 1760 and was a Chinese Official. It is said that he learned this Kata from the great Okinawan karate master Sakugawa 1733-1815 and he passed it onto the present day.

I did my Kata and received a nice bout of applause, after which some of the students commented that I was better than when I arrived and more confident in myself. This referred to the fact that I was quite shy at that time in my life.

After all the demonstrations were finished a big block of wood was brought in; at first I thought it was a training aid to make us, Kohais, suffer even more, in fact it was used to make a sweet from rice called 'Mochi'. The rice was placed in the hollowed out top of the block and hit with wooden mallets until it became a little like dough and was very sweet. It was passed around – it soon filled you up, it was accompanied by large quantities of Sake (rice wine). It wasn't long before everyone was very merry and all the masters and students present took turn in singing their favourite songs. This was not to be the end of the clubs New Year celebrations, the next evening all the clubs were to get together at a restaurant called Vikin House, for two hours you could eat and drink as much as you liked for a fixed sum of money, well, you can imagine what fifty or so fit men drank and ate! I don't think that the restaurant made a very big profit out of us. This was followed by three or four hours of non-stop drinking, needless to say I don't recall too much of the evening!

Frank demonstrates Jiyu-Gumite (Free Fighting)

Back row l-r: N. Prince, G. Thompson, K. Jones.
Front Row l-r: S. Tanabe, Unel, T. Suzuki, Frank, H. Ohtsuka, H-Bo,
Arakawa - All Japan Party.

Left to right: Master Inoue, Frank and Ikegaya Sensei.

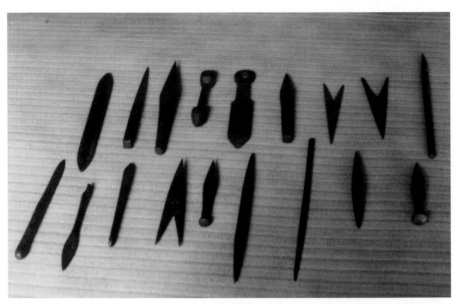

Shuriken

Shuriken and other throwing darts.

Making a TV show. Frank is last on the left of back row.

Japanese garden in Tokyo.

Frank with Master Inoue.

Japanese ladies at a shrine.

Frank practising side kick on top of a Tokyo skyscraper.

Demonstration at Meiji Shrine. Frank is the one in the middle.

Spot the steps! Ninja steps to Inoue Dojo.

Looking from the other direction.

Frank in Inoue's Dojo with kama.

Mountains of Japan.

TCP club members practising. (Note: students names on wall on small cards).

Frank running barefoot in Tokyo.

Training for my 2nd Dan

After the New Year I went back to training, I felt much more at home and everyone seemed to want to help me to improve. The training was about the same as the first lesson. The last hour would be Kata that would be anything from the nine basic Kata's of Wado-Ryu: These being the five Pinan Katas said to have been made by Yasutsune Itosu (1830 – 1914). Together with Ku-Shanku; Naifanchi and Sieshan, both of which use tension in parts of these two Katas to help you to learn how to control your muscles, an important part of Wado-Ryu Karate and Chinto a very quick change of technique and direction make this a very difficult Kata to perform. As well as Kata we would practice Kihon Kumite, basic sparring of Wado-Ryu, these techniques are a very important part of training in how you can use your body to avoid an opponents attack and utilise his power to your advantage. Created by Master Ohtsuka early on in his development of Wado-Ryu they teach the students the ideas of traditional martial arts. There are ten basic Kihon Kumite used in the grading of students in Wado-Ryu but there are many more techniques of this kind learnt by advance students of Wado-Ryu which are very dangerous and not generally known. Whenever we did free sparring the last hour would go so fast that lots of students used to stay on after class to do some more training. During one of these sparring sessions I ended up with Meade Sensei after a few exchanges he got me with his favoured kick Maegeri (front kick) in the rib. The pain was so intense that I had to go down on one knee to get my breath back and to this day it was the most painful kick I have ever received. Being a bit mad at myself for being caught with a move I knew he was good at I pulled myself together and attacked him as hard as I could, hitting him right between the eyes with Tobikomizuki (snap punch) it surprised me as much as Meade. But for the first time since I had been doing Karate I felt that I could get a punch in with power and control and knew in my heart that if I had not controlled it I would have knocked him flat. After the lesson Meade put his hand on my shoulder and said "Good Frank San", (San is almost like Mr in English and is a polite form of address). It was obvious this punch was a good move for me and I needed to practice it until it came as sharp as a blade.

One of the sparring practices that I was not too keen on was when Kyu grades (below black belt) attacked the black belts as hard as they could without control. The Dan grades were to only block and not attack back, it was almost impossible to stop everything and the black belts would very often come off the worse for wear. One night we were training in this kind of sparring when I came up against a brown belt which some of the students called 'Jaws' because he had all his front teeth knocked out and replaced by silver ones.

This night he must have decided to show me that a Japanese brown belt was too good for an English black belt. Knowing that I was only supposed to block he went all out for the kill, he tried everything that he could think of. When he got in close head butts, elbows, knees and all as hard as he could I could see that if this went on much longer I was going to end up like Jaws with all silver teeth. After a little while my self-preservation instinct took over and as he moved in I hit him in the head with Mawashgeri, knocking him senseless. I was feeling quite pleased with myself, but this was not to last for long, the class was stopped and in an angry voice Meade sensei said I had not done a thing right since I had been there, and was ordered to stay behind after class and clean the dojo out and in particularly the toilets. I bowed and took my punishment like a man, but inside I felt like breaking Jaws neck.

A few weeks after my encounter with Jaws I entered the Dojo to find Arakawa sensei pinning on the wall a notice that a Dan grading was to be held some ten days later, he said that it would be possible for me to take a second Dan if I trained hard. Meada Sensei told me not to worry and to train as hard as I could. Over the next ten days I spent all my time in the club and almost trained myself to a standstill. The grading was to be held at a High School, I went along with some other students from the club who were taking 1st and 3rd Dan. When we arrived there was already a large amount of Karate-ka (karate students) warming up. The grades being taken that day were from 1st to 4th Dan. After a little while the grading examiners came in, this was the first shock of the day, there were twelve including the founder of Wado-Ryu Ohtsuka O Sensei, his son Jiro Sensei, now head of Wado-Ryu and many older men that I had never seen before. It made me feel nervous just looking at them never mind doing the grading. I sat down on the floor with the rest of the students and watched the first kyu students taking their black belt. I could see that the Nich Dia (top university club for Wado-Ryu) and the T.P.C. brown belts were the sharpest and that gave me some encouragement. My mind drifted back to when I took my 1st Dan, that day 67 Karate-ka took part and only seven passed, I wonder if it could possibly be worse. After some time I was called up to do my basic punches, Chinto Kata and Kihon kumite, then free sparring. I had never fought or seen my opponent before, so I had no idea of his capabilities but the last few months had hardened my belief in myself and from the start I attacked him without mercy and not going back an inch. I remember he only scored on me once in the whole fight. When Yama (stop) was called and I could have hit myself for relaxing too quickly. We bowed and went to get changed then sat down together to watch the 2nd and 3rd Dans do their examination. After all the Dan gradings were ended the examiners went off to discuss the merits of the applicants and after a little while returned to make their announcement. My partner and myself had passed, we shook hands and went to pay our grading fee. Before we went Master Ohtsuka gave a small talk and demonstration of what he thought many of them were doing wrong. All the students from the club had passed. One had passed 3rd Dan, as Senpai (senior) he offered to buy us a drink to celebrate. We all went to a ryoriya (Japanese style eating house), this was one day that being a Kohai (junior) was an advantage!

The Senpai Kohai relationship in martial arts is very important, but is little understood by western students of martial arts. To put this relationship into words is difficult, but I will try. It is impossible to continue to improve your standard in martial arts if you do not respect your seniors, their achievements in the past is knowledge of martial arts and life will be of great value to you in your study. 99% of Karate must be passed on by word of mouth and through experience, that means that without seniors passing on their knowledge to you, you just cannot improve. If you are not respectful to your elders, human nature as it is, will naturally not wish to help you as much as he or she would if you were more respectful, and soon you start to fall behind your equals. "Little things mean a lot", is an old English saying, this saying applies very well to the Senpai Kohai relationship. Helping your Senpai with small things and respecting him when he is there and when he is not will, from my experience, make you a better person and martial artist. In return the Senpai should act as he would wish his student to act, he should dress and act respectfully and talk respectfully. It is not just coincidence that bad mannered students have had bad mannered instructors.

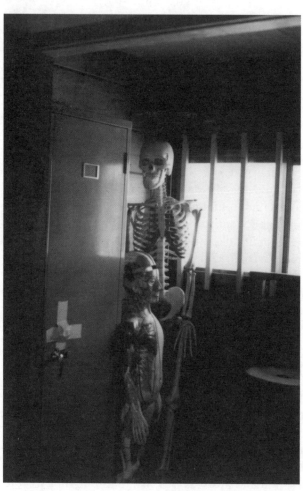

Vital points practice dummies, or is it a student that didn't make his grade?

Traditional Wado-Ryu

Wado-Ryu is a fast style of Karate that does not rely on power alone to defeat an aggressor. This point is important if the practitioner wants to continue to improve into old age, as your strength diminishes, deflections and evasion will play a more important part in defeating an aggressor.

From the beginning of Wado-Ryu, Master Ohtsuka emphasised that power should not be met with power, but the power of his attack harnessed and used to defeat him. Nagashizuki is a technique that shows this aspect of Wado-Ryu well. Nagashi (swept away), Zuki (punch) is used to counter an attack and is practiced with great intensity in Wado-Ryu. It is not uncommon to spend thirty minutes in a lesson practicing Nagashizuki and moves coming from it, such as step back Nagashizuki, or performing a punch or kick before hand. Nagashizuki is one of the six basic punches practised at the start of each lesson in a traditional Wado-Ryu dojo. The basic stance which Nagashizuki is practised from is called Hidari shizntai (Hidari)-(left) and (shizentai)-(natural). If you start walking as you naturally do and stop as your left foot touches the ground this will be very close to the natural stance of Wado-Ryu. Migi shizental (Migi – right) is used when you are going to punch Nagashizuki with your right hand.

From Shizentai stance you move forward as the attacker begins his move, twisting your body and hips to accelerate the punch and avoid the incoming kick, punch, knife or whatever and with your forward fist punch into the face. Nagashizuki is widely used by experienced practitioners of Wado-Ryu.

Basic techniques are the foundation on which the art of traditional Wado-Ryu is built, they are the building blocks for a strong spirit, legs, arms and body. A saying I well remember from Japan is "If the foundations of your house are bad your house will fall down, if the foundations of your Karate are bad, you will be knocked down". The first basic punch practised in Japan is Junzuki, (Jun – front, and Zuki – punch) this is a complex punch that involves years of constant practice to master. It is said that Junzuki has the power to break the rib cage of a man with one single blow. The punch uses a propelling of the body forward by means of a big step to greatly increase its power, at the point of impact the front knee is bent, the hips are kept low, the back leg is extended out behind you with the foot flat on the floor; the punch is practised at body height. In basics called "Chudan" all the six basic punches start from the hip and go out in a straight line with the fist knuckles pointing downwards, at the last split-second before hitting the target the fist is spun over, this movement greatly increases the speed at the last seconds, thus adding to the power.

The scientific and physical dynamics of Junzuki are very complex, but it is for all that very much a natural move. If you have ever tried to push a car you have no doubt found yourself in a Junzuki stance, as it only takes a few seconds of pushing to realise that with your hips low and your one foot well in front of the other you will get far more power to move the car. It is interesting how early Masters of Karate devised such a punch, it may well have been that one day they were pushing a cart out of the mud, such an idea may sound laughable today but most techniques have small beginnings and are built on over the years.

In a four-hour lesson in Japan we spent around fifteen minutes on Junzuki. For more advanced students a kick is added before the punch, nearly always Maegri (front kick). All the basics are preformed up and down the room. The Instructors shout out the words "Mawatte Jodan Uke" when it is necessary to turn back down the room: "Mawatte" means turn 180 degrees and "Jodan-uke" head block, this is executed by stepping across with your rear foot and at the same time you turn blocking up with your forward arm to stop an imaginary punch to your face: sometimes it was not imaginary as the Instructor would sneak up behind you and when you turned he would punch to your face. The first time this was done to me in Japan I missed the punch completely and ended up with a big lump on my forehead, needless to say I learned to block a lot quicker after that.

Sometimes all the time allotted to basics was spent on just one of the techniques. Spending an hour or so on just one technique for someone young and fit this is more mentally tiring then physically tiring, and this mental training is one of the most important aspects of the traditional side in Japan. The Instructors are trying to strengthen your spirit for real combat. Very often when doing this kind of training the Instructor would walk around the students with a Shinai, this is a bamboo practise sword used in the Japanese art of Kendo (the way of the sword). He would prod the students into the right positions, or, if he thought you were not putting your all into training, give you a few taps with it to waken you up a little. This way of instructing is very much the Japanese way of teaching and is inbuilt into their culture. While in the West it is common for Instructors to praise their students for their good work this is not the case in Japan. Often the better you are the more the Instructor would scold you to try to push you to even higher standards; it makes your life a lot easier if you can understand that he does not necessarily shout at you because he doesn't like you but because he does like you, this is very difficult for Western students to appreciate. Fortunately, I was instructed by Japanese from the beginning so I did understand this a little better than most of the students coming to the T.P.C. from abroad. Many of whom only attended two or three times at the Club, never to be seen there again.

Gyakuzuki, Gyaku (reverse) Zuki (punch) is the second basic punch. Reverse punch as the word implies is a punch which uses the opposite arm to the leg, for example, if your left leg is forward you will punch with your right arm. More hip is used in Gyakuzuki, this is possible as the stance is a little wider, giving more scope to twist your hip. The punch is aimed at the body. Advanced students practise Maegri with the same punch, on turning to go back up the room a low sweeping block called "Gedan barai", gedan (low) barai (sweep) is used. Often the Instructors would kick at your stomach as you turned, they would do this to see if you were blocking correctly.

All the basics of Wado-Ryu require the students to keep their hips low, one of the ways practised in Japan to help strengthen the hips was to have someone sitting on your shoulders as you practised Junzuki and Gyakuzuki going up and down the room. Ten minutes of this and my hips would feel as if they were on fire and my legs would be shaking. Another way to strengthen your hips is by standing in Shikodachi, this is a technique used a great deal in Sumo for hip strengthening. Shiko in Sumo involves raising each leg in turn as high as possible and bringing it down as hard as humanly possible, and stamping the foot on the ground. Shiko is performed as part of the ritual at the beginning of each Sumo bout, the power of the Sumo wrestler's hips will testify to the excellency of this technique. Shikodachi stance in Karate involves spreading your feet around four feet apart, your hips down low – as low as knee height, in some training both feet are turned out at to angle of 45 degrees, the idea is to stay in this position for as long as possible. Most Westerners start to feel pain in their hips and legs after about thirty or forty seconds. I well remember a new Japanese student being made to stand in Shikodachi for the whole of the first lesson, whilst at the same time being instructed how to punch correctly. In general, Japanese students seem to have stronger hips than the Westerners at the beginning of their Karate training, we do catch up with them, but it takes a few years. I have no doubt that very few Westerners in their first lesson could have stood for more than a few minutes in Shikodachi.

"Junzuki-no-Tsukkomi", Tsukkomi meaning Lean lunge, is the third basic punch and is used to attack the face. It uses a lunging forward action to increase power and distance of the punch. At the point of impact your front leg is bent, your body leaning from the waist and in Mahanmi, side viewing stance, which means your body is sideways on impact. This has the advantage of cutting down on the area that is visible to your opponent. The turn on this basic is the same as Junzuki.

"Gyakuzuki-no-Tsukkomi", reverse leaning forward punch, is aimed at the lower part of the body. The distance between the feet for this punch is wider than all other punching stances in Wado-Ryu basics and is around twice the width of your shoulders. At the point of impact your forward leg bears around eighty percent of your weight, with your back leg straight and toes pointing slightly inwards and inline with the back heel of the forward foot. The turn is the same as Gyakuzuki Gedan barai. Both Tsukkomi punches are practised with Maegri front kick by advanced students.

The final two punches practised at the start of training in Japan are, "Nagashizuki", which I have referred to at the beginning of this chapter and "Tomikomizuki", which is my favourite punch. This punch can be said to be near to a straight boxing punch, but it is far more interesting. From the same stance as Nagashizuki (Hidari shizentai) you slide forward with your foot bringing both arms up together you punch out with your forward leaning arm, whilst the other arm finishes on your chest, after hitting the target you pull your hand back in a snapping action, very much like a boxing punch. This technique can be delivered at great speed, especially using a big step forward called "Zenshinshite" and is a very powerful punch delivered to the face.

After basics we would usually have a short rest, but before this well-earned breather, it is custom to do basic kicks. On the whole we did not spend as long on kicking techniques. The secret of performing good kicks is to be flexible in the hips. To see that students became flexible the instructors in Japan employed some pretty horrific stretching exercises, if you were unlucky and had stiff hips it could be very painful. They included sitting on the floor with the soles of your feet together and someone standing on your knees, pressing them downwards to the floor, or sitting with your legs as far apart as possible whereupon your partner pushes you forward in an attempt to get your chest to touch the floor; whilst these kind of stretching exercises were going on one very often heard moans and groans of pain.

In Japan it was considered that around ten minutes for each hours training should be set aside for stretching, warming up and strengthening of the joints and body. Some old methods of strengthening the legs for kicking are still quite popular today in Japan. The most popular of these is kicking with iron clogs on the your feet called "tetsu-geta", it is traditional to tie them on to your feet by means of a karate belt. You need a pair of geta that are not too heavy, some of the geta at the T.P.C. weighed about seven pounds, far too heavy for me and it was a real struggle to get them off the ground. Normally geta training would be done at the same time as "Makiware" training, padded post practice, spending around fifteen minutes on each.

There are four kinds of kicks practised above all others in Japanese Wado-Ryu Club. They are basics of kicking which all new students are grounded. They are as follows:- "Maegri", front kick "Mawashigeri", roundhouse kick, "Sokutogeri" side kick and "Ushirogeri", back kick. All of these kicks start by bringing the knee up to stomach height, this has the advantage of not letting your opponent know which of the kicks you are about to execute until the last second in combat; this gives you the element of surprise. There are many applications for these four kicks used in competition and free sparring in Europe. Many are given points in tournaments of which in real combat would not knock out the aggressor. In Japan more time is spent on the basic kicks to get them sufficiently powerful enough to stop the aggressor in his tracks. Maegri uses the ball of the foot as the contact point, your toes are bent back as not to damage them, using the hips to generate the power. Maegri can be used on an opponent's body from shin height to face level. My favourite attack for Maegri is to the shin, as I am only 5 feet 5 inches tall my opponents have great difficulty in doing anything about it. I practice the kick by placing a kick bag against the wall and kicking at it around eighteen inches off the ground, this helps to build up the muscles used in this kick. In all kicks of Wado-Ryu the foot must be returned to the ground as soon as possible as you are at your most vulnerable when standing on one leg. Sokuto-geri uses the side of the foot as the contact point. Beginners in Japan usually start by practising "Sokuto Fumikomi", stamping kick. This is used to attack the knee joint area and also to stamp down on the fallen opponents. When mastered, it can be used to the face or body. This kick is not seen very much in competition, as it is difficult to control and referees are reluctant to give any kind of score for it. Mawashigeri uses the instep and ball of the foot as contact point. The ball of the foot is quite often used for attacking the body in Japan and the instep is used for groin and face. This is a very popular competition kick in Europe to the face, in Japan it is not so commonly seen. As the word "Mawashigeri", round house kick, implies the kick comes from the side in an attempt to get round your opponents defences. "Ushirogeri", back kick, is the fourth of the basic kicks. It involves turning your back on your opponent for a split second before kicking backwards, using your heel as a contact point. This kick is not commonly used above the body height in Wado-Ryu and great care must be taken with it. It is difficult to keep your balance and is never the best idea to turn your back on your opponent.

At the club we had a large bag for kicking. Kicking Maegri is not too difficult. Sensei Murase used to kick the bag so hard with Maegri that it sometimes hit the ceiling. Sokutogeri is not so easy to practice on the bag. The best man I ever saw for this was an American named Benny Urquidez, nick named "The Jet" he was the American Kick Boxing Champion and was in Japan at the same time as myself. He was there to fight some Japanese kick boxers, all of whom he flattened. He was practising a short distance from my Club, I went to visit his dojo, where there was quite a large crowd. Urquidez was kicking the bag so hard with Mawashigeri that it was bending in half. He then did a one-step Sokutogeri, breaking the strap holding the bag to the ceiling and sending it around twenty feet down the room.

The problem with kicking too hard on a bag with bare feet is that it can bruise your feet. I noticed that Urquidez was using training shoes when he was putting all his power into it. Whenever I practice kicking on the bag I use training shoes, especially for Mawashigeri, as your instep has many blood vessels near the surface and they can be easily damaged. The title of this chapter is Traditional Wado-Ryu, therefore it is appropriate that I should end it with an insight into traditional sparring. Today one can purchase any martial art magazine to find it filled with tournament reports and competition news. It is very easy to forget that Karate was developed in the first place to give the practitioner a better chance to survive in the fight for his life. Karate is not a game, and any method or technique which gives you a better chance of walking away the victor must be studied with the utmost seriousness.

In Japan many students have taken competition sparring to their heart, especially the young, which is understandable, but fortunately many of the older students and Masters still practice the old ways of sparring and its techniques. If you are interested in the old ways you can still find Masters who can put you on the right track. These Masters usually have a wealth of stories and tips on traditional Karate methods and I have included some of the tips and stories throughout this book, but to follow are some points within the realms of decency, in the hope that it will give you a better understanding in this way of fighting off the competition floor.

- Be honest with yourself; understand your weaknesses and strengths. Do not be fooled into thinking your technique is good when in your heart you know it isn't. Your adversary will not let it pass if your actions are weak and ineffective, he will take advantage of your foolishness. Be honest about your fears of combat and bring them out into the open so as to overcome them. Do not push them into the back of your mind, otherwise they may come forward when you are in real combat and break up your rhythm.

- When you attack you should attack with great spirit, go in without mercy and have no regard for your adversaries feelings, and crush his spirit. When you have him on the run you should not give him time to recover his spirit. Try to drive your opponent into positions that will make him uneasy, such as against a wall, or some other object in the room. If you are out of doors drive him into uneven ground, or into bushes etc., in an attempt to break up his fighting rhythm and concentration. If he falls by accident be cautious of going in immediately to finish him off as he may be ready for your attack. Wait until he is getting up then attack hard and crush him when his mind will be on rising.

- During combat you will sometimes get the feeling that your opponent has lost his mind, in the sense that he is caught in two minds. When you get this feeling you should attack instantly before he can regain his thoughts, you must learn to recognise such feeling and use them to your own advantage.

- Learn to harness your temper and channel it into your techniques.

- You must master moves of attack and defence which require no conscious thought, as at times there is not time for such thoughts.

- Timing and distancing is the key to the mastery of combat, study this well.

- Learn from others, but develop your own fighting patterns.

- You must understand the spirit of not going back too much and the spirit of standing your ground.

- Learn to master your voice to help you defeat your opponent and look in their eyes to install fear in them.

- Do not expect your adversary to be fair. Be prepared for anything, you must learn to think in terms of real combat and not competition sparring.

The following stories told to me in Japan highlight timing and distancing. Being prepared for anything and not thinking as in competition:- Timing and distancing by experts of the martial arts is always something to marvel at. When I think of distancing and timing I often think of Master Ohtsuka, even at 87 years of age he was doing demonstrations against an opponent wielding a samuari sword, to do a demonstration of this kind the timing and distancing must be perfect or serious injury could occur. One of the stories popular in Japan is about when Master Ohtsuka fought a duel against a sword wielding Kendo expert who had challenged him, he calmly bided his time waiting for the Kendo expert to attack, as the attack came he timed his counter exactly sweeping him off his feet using perfect distancing and timing.

One evening I went to a Club in Yokohoma to train with some of the students whom I had met during training in Tokyo. The Senior Instructor at the club was a forth Dan who had been practising Wado-Ryu Karate for around twenty years. He told me an interesting story which sums up the saying "be prepared for anything". When he was a young student in the early sixties he went on a weekend training camp. At the camp there was a third Dan of quiet disposition, at the end of the first days training the Instructors requested everyone to pair up for free sparring. He noticed one of the students was being carried off by the Instructors in a state of unconsciousness, and the quiet third Dan looking distinctly worried. At the end of the next days training when free sparring was called for by the Instructors he found himself paired with the quiet third Dan. No sooner had the sparring started the quiet third Dan took him completely by surprise by spitting in his face, followed immediately by a punch to the chin knocking him off the ground. Certainly this behaviour is totally unacceptable in competitions, and no doubt rather dirty. However, in traditional combat you should be prepared for anything.

———

For full insight into fighting techniques see
Wado-Ryu Karate Fighting Techniques Uncovered.

Six Principles of Kata

1. Kata must be alive, done with feeling and purpose.

2. Kata must be performed with spirit.

3. Changes in application of power, techniques, can be strong or yielding, hard then soft.

4. Variation in the timing of movement, sometimes fast, sometimes slow.

5. Proper rhythm of breathing, when to breath in and when to breath out.

6. Maintaining proper balance.

Kata, the Soul of Wado-Ryu

Kata is said to be the soul of Karate and, to a traditionalist it almost becomes a religious rite when performed. Kata is performed alone and involves the pre-arranged movements of attack and defence, which have been passed down from Karate and martial arts experts of old, each Kata begins with a defensive move, emphasising that Karate is a defensive art which should be used for good not evil.

Kata's of Karate are shrouded in mystery and hidden techniques, each move within the Kata may have four or more hidden movements. It is important for these reasons that a student should be instructed by a High Master within the Ryu (style school) who has learned the Kata's off to a fine art. The learning of these hidden movements is a lifetime of study but great fun for traditional Karate-ka.

Wado-Ryu Katas bring the practitioner near to past masters, who have left the worldly bounds of this life, but have left their words and thoughts in the techniques they left behind, and through the practice of Kata we almost go back as if through a time warp.

Wado-Ryu Katas should be performed with spirit. The movements of the Katas are against multiple opponents of four upwards. Some of the defences are against weapons, such as the bo (staff). In the minds eye of an experienced practitioner, as he performs the Kata these men and weapons confront him as if they were really there.

In Karate there are three main kinds of Kata practised: Nahate, Tomarite and Shurite. These refer to areas of Okinawa where these styles were most practised. Wado-Ryu is mostly Shurite, which has fast light movements over the ground culminating in a powerful attack or defence. Master Hironori Ohtsuka changed some of the movements to help students learn about the old martial arts of Japan and included jujitsu techniques (locks etc). These he passed on to his most senior students. The jujitsu techniques of Wado-Ryu Katas are very complex and most students in the West do not have any in-depth knowledge of these. Wado-Ryu still uses the names passed down through centuries such as Jion, Jitte, Niseishi, Wanshu, Bassai and Rohai. Many of these words refer to men's names, and a lot of these words have a Chinese influence.

The core of the Kata system are Pinan Katas one to five, these five Katas are the building blocks for the more advanced Katas. They are the ones most practised in Japan. There is a saying in Japan "Kata hitotsu sannen" this means "It takes three years to learn one Kata". Although most students start to realise that this is not long enough, and that it is a lifetime struggle.

Kata, because of the complexity of the movement, needs to be practised many thousand of times. It was not uncommon to practise one Kata twenty or thirty times one after the other until the movements of the Kata became automatic, like changing gear on the car. When you have a good understanding of a Kata you sometimes get to the end of the Kata and wonder if you have missed out parts of it. This happens when you do the Kata without your mind being involved with the movements. Of course this is impossible as your mind is involved with everything you do, yet this is the feeling that you get. Yet for advanced students many masters feel this is not good for real combat for you to be involved in a movement without thinking may leave you open to danger. To risk victory on an automatic response when your life is in danger of being lost can be too large a risk to take. This is why advanced students of Karate try to control their minds from being lost in performing that Kata. This is a constant struggle, yet it is very important not to loose the feeling of real combat when performing that Kata. These complex readings of Kata and the struggle to control ones mind is one of the main reasons why many of the top Wado-Ryu exponents have become interested in Zen Buddhisim, in the hope that it will help their mind and in so doing improve their combat skills.

Mokuso (empty mind) training is practised at the start of many classes in Japan. This involves sitting in Seiza (on your knees with your bottom resting on your heels – insteps flat on the floor) and your back straight. The idea is to try and rid your mind of all conscious thoughts. It is very difficult and needs years of practise, sometimes you get there, and for a few seconds you feel free from the problems of this world, but soon your worldly thoughts would return. When practising Mokuso, the Instructor would walk around to see that all the students backs are straight and if not would lightly touch you on the shoulder, this indicated you should bend forward slightly, whereupon you would be struck three or four times across the shoulders with a Shinai (bamboo practise sword) to remind you not to do it again. Whatever you might think about this kind of harsh treatment there can be no doubt that if a person is of equal skill and weight, the victor will be the one with the strongest mind.

It is possible to train at a Zen Temple in Japan. During my time in Japan I met an English girl who had come to try and do just that, she was told that if she stayed for one week in the Temple she would be instructed free for one month. The week involved no speaking and sitting down with her feet crossed in the lotus position, back straight, trying to clear her mind of any outside influences. Each hour she was allowed to get up and walk around or go to the toilet for a few minutes, three times a day she was given a bowl of rice and some water. After three days she had to give up as her legs were paining her so much. If you have ever tried sitting down without moving for any length of time you will have no doubt felt something like she felt, it is extremely difficult thing to do.

The first Kata learned is Pinan Nidan. Pinan (peace) Nidan (level two) Pinan Katas were arranged by the famous Okinawan Karate Master, Yatsutune Itosu, 1830 – 1914. It appears that around the year 1904 Karate was introduced into the schools curriculum in Okinawa. It was felt at the time that the more advanced Katas practised at that time were a little too difficult to commence with, so Itosu introduced the Pinan system into Karate to help bridge the gap.

Pinan-nidan has twenty one moves which are first practised individually then in combinations of attack and defence. It takes around twenty five seconds to perform.

Although Nidan is number two Kata, it is practised first, this is because it is considered easier for new students to understand as many of the punches and blocks are learned in the basics. The Kata is characterised by the beginning when you counter an attack coming in from the left, with bottom fist block (tettsui) at the same time as dropping the weight of the body to increase the power of the block. The Kata finishes with two spear hand attacks (nukite) to the kidney area.

Pinan –Shodan (level one) this Kata is more difficult, for it has Shuto-uke (knife hand block) included. This block is extremely difficult technically to perform correctly. Master Ohtsuka described it as one of the most difficult moves in Wado-Ryu and said it would take twenty years before the students would understand it correctly. The block is repeated seven times throughout the Kata and involves blocking with the side of your hand, the incoming punch to the face as you block your body twists in the opposite direction. At the point of the block your stance is 'Mahanmi Nekoashi', side viewing cat stance. Shodan has twenty six moves and takes around twenty five seconds to perform.

Pinan-sandan (level three) has twenty two moves, and takes approximately twenty five seconds to perform. It is characterised by a double block, done in unison at the start and three elbow blocks.

Pinan-yodan (level four) is a very nice flowing Kata and is very often the Kata many Wado-Ryu students like best. It has a rather unusual ending for a Karate Kata, in so much as the movements are very representative of Tai-chi (Chinese martial art) movements. The movements are called 'Kaketa' and means grabbing or hooking the arm or wrist. The technique is proceeded by a movement which represents pulling the attackers head down onto the knee and then turning round quickly to execute Kaketa on the attackers punching arm. Yodan has twenty seven moves and takes approximately twenty eight seconds to perform.

Pinan-Godan (level five) is characterised by a jump into the air to avoid staff attack to the legs, it has fast changes of direction and complex hand movements. These points combine to make it a spectacular Kata to watch. It can take two or three years before a student begins to learn Godan. In Japan there does not seem to be any rush to go from one Kata to the next, this is not always the case in European clubs.

I recall one of the students in Japan that I had met who had been practising Kata for fifteen years and only knew nine-Kata! He was quite happy not to learn any more until he felt his Instructor thought he was ready to learn any more. I feel that the attitude of the Japanese in this is why the students of Kata in Japan is much better than in Europe. Kata is the search for self perfection of ones mind and body, it is a fight against ones self to master its complexities and inner meanings. A Kata exponent is like wine, he improves with age in technique and mind.

Osaka Castle

For full insight into Wado-Ryu Kata see
The Complete Art Uncovered or Wado-Ryu Karata Kata Uncovered.

Master Hironori Ohtsuka
1892 - 1982

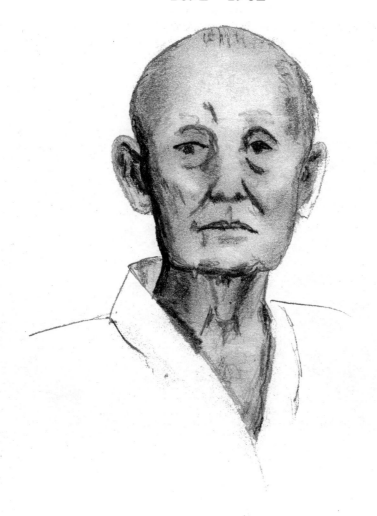

A Hawkis '05

Memories of Master Hironori Ohtsuka

Master Ohtsuka was the founder of Wado-Ryu Karate and the man whom I most wanted to train under in Japan. Ohtsuka was in his late seventies when I first met him in England. He regularly visited the T.P.C. Club as well as instructing classes there he also did private lessons for visiting Wado-Ryu instructors.

Master Ohtsuka was born in Ibaragi-ken, some one hundred miles from Tokyo on the 1st June, 1892. His father was a Doctor of Medicine. He began his study of Martial Arts in 1897 under the ju-jitsu teacher, Chojiro Ebashi. His study of Shindo-Yoshin Ryu Ju Jitsu started in 1905 under Tatsusabura Nakayama, who was the top Instructor at that time in Japan. Many parents of good families had their sons instructed in some kind of Martial Art as part of their education.

In 1910 Ohtsuka entered Waseda University, where he studied commerce. He continued to study different styles of Martial Arts and broaden his outlook.

In June 1921 he was awarded his graduation certificate in Shindo-Yoshin Ryu Ju Jitsu, around the time of Ohtsuka receiving this Masters certificate, a lot of interest in the new art, of Karate as it was going to be called, had been started, by exhibitions of the Art of Karate in Tokyo by Gichin Funakoshi and others, the most famous of these exhibitions being the one given for Prince Hirohito on the 6th June 1921.

Ohtsuka heard about this new art and went to visit Funakoshi, and he became one of his first students. By 1928 he was assistant Instructor at

Funakoshi's Dojo. His body movements were superb, flowing from one technique to another without any effort at all. One of Master Ohtsukas sayings was that you should try to move like a man of eighty without effort or tenseness. He regularly did demonstrations with his son Jiro Ohtsuka, now headmaster of Wado-Ryu (Ohtsuka O sensei died in February 1982). I would describe his son as a real Samurai, when ever I saw him he would be sitting bolt upright and at the time had a short crew hair cut, a well built man and had a very similar body movement as his father. One day, I went to the club to find the Chief Instructor for Wado-Ryu in Europe, Master Tatsuo Suzuki, free sparring a seventh Dan under the watchful eye of Grand Master Ohtsuka. Master Suzuki fought superbly well and was really too much for his seventh Dan opponent. On many occasions I arrived at the club to find Master Ohtsuka instructing some individual or group. On one occasion Ohtsuka came out of the changing room with his Karate suit, some of the black belts offered to put it into a small bag that Master Ohtsuka carried. For about five minutes they tried in vain to get the suit into the bag, after folding it up, unfolding it, pushing and shoving to try to get it all in they gave up. All this time Ohtsuka was looking at them with a kind of fatherly expression, when he could see that they had given up he quickly folded the suit up, slipped it into the bag and zipped it up to the utter amazement of the black belts and the laughter of all the other students. Even in the folding of a suit Master Ohtsuka was supreme. He stressed the importance of training every day for life and to try and improve your mind as well as your body. I feel very happy that I could spend some of my time in this world with such a great Master of Martial Arts.

For full in-depth history of Wado-Ryu see
Wado-Ryu Karate the Complete Art Uncovered.

Away from Karate

Although my training schedule and work kept me very busy I tried to look at other things whenever I had a day off. Tokyo is a massive City of many contrasts where the modern world and the old world live side by side. Shopping in Tokyo is an experience which all foreigners find quite exhilarating; department stores for example are enormous and sell everything you could possibly want including English and European food and sweets, but were all very expensive. As you entered these massive stores there would be uniformed ladies standing at the escalators welcoming you to the store and wiping the hand rail for you as you stepped on. Many shoppers carried their shopping in a kind of cloth, called a 'Furoshiki'. Japanese like to buy their food every day so shops were always busy. The service in the shops in Japan was first class. In the main shopping areas of Tokyo, such as Shinjuku, where a lot of young people go there would be many arcades with slot machines and wherever you go in Tokyo there are Pachinko pinball halls; Pachinko is a game that I believe most Westerners do not spend the time to work out and therefore don't realise the fun there is in it. On entering the Pachinko hall you buy a quantity of balls and feed them into the machine, with a lever you flick them into holes of different values, if you get them into the high value holes you receive more balls to flick again. If you gain enough balls you can exchange them for a prize. There are, so I was told, professional Pachinko players that make a good living doing it.

Japanese love good food and this is reflected in the wide variety of high class restaurants all over Tokyo. I don't think I would be going too far in saying it probably is one of the best places in the world to find so many first class restaurants. One of the places I often visited just to sit down and get a bit of peace and quiet was the Japanese Coffee House, I usually had my breakfast there for around £1.50, you would get a coffee, toast, an egg and a small towel hot in winter and cold in summer to freshen you up.

The parks are one of the few places that are green in Tokyo and are nearly always full of people, especially on Sundays when people would sit on the grass and have a picnic. In Spring time, when the cherry blossom was out, the parks would be full of parties of people who would sit down under the trees and celebrate the coming of Spring. Spring and Autumn was a lovely time to walk in the parks and countryside.

Most parks have a Shinto shrine and while there I would watch the worshippers worshipping. It is simply clapping hands, bowing and ringing a bell. On festivals large amounts of money was thrown into the shrine and food and drink was offered. Stalls and amusements are set up leading to the shrine and there is very much a party atmosphere.

One of the temples that I went to visit was the Sengakuji temple, this temple is famous all over Japan as the resting place of the forty seven Samurais. This true story is well worth telling, it happened in 1702. Naganori Asano, lord of Ako castle and a man known for his goodness, unable to endure the persistently unfair treatment which he received from Yoshinaka Kira, the official overseer of ceremonies and a man of mean intent, drew his sword in protest against the latter in the Imperial castle of Edo. Because of this deed Lord Asano was sentenced to death by disembowelment by the shogunate. His faithful retainers deeply discontented with this sentencing made a plea to the shogunate for Asano's re-establishment, but they were unable to succeed in their endeavour.

Yoshitaka Oishi, chief retainer of the Asano clan and forty seven other loyal retainers rebelling against this political corruption and the government's inadequate measures, decided after long thought to avenge the death of their Lord. After much planning, at midnight, on December 14th 1702, they raided the mansion of Lord Kira and after a battle with Kira's Samurais they seized and beheaded him. Their deed not only avenged the death of their lord but calmed the mounting discontent among the people toward the government. Abiding by the law of the Country they courageously took their own lives, on the February of the next year their remains were buried beside the tomb of their lord, and to this day the tale of the heroic deeds is handed down from generation to generation. This true story is just one of many which Japanese people are brought up on.

Nearly every night on television there is a Samurai film or something relating to their traditional Samurai past. Families with a Samurai past are rightly proud of it. The Japanese family is a very tight knit and very often the grandfather and grandmother will live with their sons and daughters even after they are married and help look after their grand-children. I was invited many times to Japanese homes and was treated with the utmost courtesy. When invited it is the custom to bring some kind of small gift, like sweets usually wrapped in nice paper.

Many homes usually have one room furnished in the traditional Japanese style. It may have in the corner a shrine to their dead relatives. Electrical items such as hi-fi's and T.V.'s take up a lot of room. Most Japanese rooms are separated by sliding screens. They don't usually have separate bedrooms but at night they just pull out of cupboards built into the wall a futon mattress and sleep on the floor, it is very warm and comfortable. Most homes have a small bath. Bathing is almost a ritual in Japan and if you don't have one at home there is the public bath house that usually has several pools of different temperatures, from warm to boiling hot. The Japanese must be the cleanest people in the world as most bath once or twice a day!

Food is usually eaten on a low table sitting on Japanese cushions called 'Zabuton'. On the health side Japanese eat a good diet low in fat; heart attacks, generally a big killer in the West are very rare in Japan. The life span for the average Japanese is well into their eighties, their main health problem seems to be their stomach. Some people seem to think that it may be connected to the Japanese passion for pickles, lots of salt and raw fish – Sashimi. Raw sliced fish is not eaten as much as some people in the West think, the most popular being tunny squid, sea bream and sea bass. Another dish I was often given when visiting was Tempura, this is vegetables, fish, or really anything coated in batter and deep fried. Meat is very expensive in Japan so not served as often as in the West.

I have always been interested in history and Japan has a wealth of it. I visited as many of the museums as possible. Japanese museums are of a high quality and can help a lot in understanding the history of martial arts. Many paintings depict battle scenes of past centuries and most of the museums have ancient Samurai and martial arts weapons on show.

About as far from the peace of a museum you can get is an area in Tokyo called Akihabara, this is the main area in Tokyo for selling electrical goods such as T.V.'s, radios and calculators, one shop had some 200 T.V's going at the same time. If you could not find an electrical gadget there it would be doubtful if it was ever made.

If you board the train at Akihabara the next main stop is Tokyo station. The area around Tokyo station is the most expensive in Japan. As well as government offices there are many hotels and the most famous street in Japan, the Ginza, this street was the first one in Tokyo to have brick buildings. It has many expensive shops and restaurants, so it was not a place that I visited too often. A place I did visit quite often was Kamakura, this is about one hour from Tokyo and has many shrines and on the coast of Sagami Bay many Japanese people visit Kamakura just to get out of the big City and into the lovely countryside of Japan for a day.

Frank and karate students local eating house.

Looking and training in other Martial Arts

After my grading I decided to have a look at some other martial arts and have a go at one or two. When time allowed I went to many clubs and I must say I was always treated in a most respectful manner. One of the clubs I had already been to on a number of occasions was the dojo of Morio Higaonna, 7th Dan chief Instructor of the Okinawa Goju Ryu Federation, Gojo Ryu the hard and soft school of Karate. The T.P.C. club visited them on a number of occasions to practice free sparring as the clubs were not far from each other. Higaonnos Dojo was made from sheet iron and wood in places and stood next to Yoyogi railway station which resulted in the building rattling every time a train went by. The club was much bigger than the T.P.C. and had around 800 students. Higaonna who lived next to the dojo was a fanatic at his own training. I only saw him once without his Karate suit on. The first thing I noticed about him was his knuckles; they were black and bleeding from the edges from his Makiwara training. His wrists were enormous and seemed to be the same size as his fore-arms. I found him a pleasant man to talk to and without doubt the best Karate man of other styles I saw during my stay. Higaonna did not spar very often but on one of my visits I was treated to him free sparring with one of his 5th Dans. To say he was a traditional fighter would, I feel, be an under estimation. Higaonna kicked him in the groin followed by grabbing him by the hair and poking him in the eyes. The poor old 5th Dan deciding he was going to loose anyway attacked front kick full power, which resulted in him being punched on the leg leaving him poleaxed on the ground. The T.P.C. club teamed up with Yoyogi Club to win the Tokyo club championships, after we all went to a little restaurant for a celebration. It was a great night out with students of different styles, I found them all nice men who reflected on Higaonna as an Instructor of great standing.

One of the martial arts that had always looked good to me was Aikido. There are two main styles, these being Uyeshibas style and Tomiki Aikido that includes competitions in their training. I went along to the headquarters of the Uyeshibas Aikido in Tokyo to have a look. Their Dojo was an impressive building with a number of classes going on at the same time. They had a large number of students and some full time instructors. The club was a bit far to go from my flat and my time being short I decided to join the Aikido club at my club which had not long started and was the tomiki style together with some other students from the Karate club. I spent about six months doing it and went to some of their competitions as a spectator. In the competitions one student has a rubber knife and attempts to score on his opponents body whilst his opponent tries to score by putting a lock or throw on him at the same time stopping him scoring with his knife. Our instructor, a third Dan who had been their university champion who had a good grasp of English said after one of the lessons that he believed that he could defeat a Karate black belt of a similar grade. One of the T.P.C. black belts offered to accommodate him. No sooner had the fight started than the Karate man hit him in the face knocking him senseless. This, I must say, did not surprise me too much as the speed of the Wado-Ryu Karate punch is very difficult to grab or avoid, even with a good Aikido 3rd Dan. Still, I learnt one or two good moves that I still practise today and enjoyed my time doing Aikido.

I have always been interested in the history of Martial Arts and going around looking at other martial arts I began to realise that weapons played an important part in the history and development of Karate. I had seen quite a few different instructors using weapons of all kinds, but it was not until I saw a demonstration at the Budoken in Tokyo that I really became interested in learning about weapons. The man that did the demonstration and his students were outstanding and made all the other masters in weapons look just ordinary. I decided I would try to find out where his club was and what the weapons were he was using. I learned that his name was Motokatsu Inoue, headmaster of the Ryu-kyu Kobudo hozon Shinko kai (the society for the promotion and preservation of Ryu-Kyu classical martial arts) the leading authority in Japan on weapons of the Ryu-Kyu Islands. These Islands are part of Japan and are in the pacific and East China Sea, some of the Islands are nearer China than Japan and are of crucial importance in the development of martial arts as we know them today.

It was in 1478 that the banning of Ryu-Kyu Islanders from carrying swords and having anything that looked like weapons that pushed the Islanders into learning other ways of defending themselves. They developed a new fighting system, using agricultural Implements called Ryu-kyu Bujutsu (weapons of the Ryu-kyu Islands) it was this art that Master Inoue had demonstrated.

I discovered that his club was some three hours from Tokyo near a town named Shimizu, but each Tuesday he came into Tokyo to instruct at the Konno shrine Dojo. This was not far from the T.P.C. club, so the next week I went along to have a look, I was immediately impressed by his kindness and warmth of greeting. There was no sign of big headedness in any way and he was genuinely pleased that I had come to his Dojo. From that moment I knew I must try to train with him, and asked to enrol as one of his students explaining that I believed it would help me to understand more about Wado-Ryu.

Master Inoue was a fascinating man to talk with, his English was not bad and he made a real effort to learn it. Inoue had come from a great family in Japan, I think it is worth just telling you about some of his back-ground. His Grandfather, Katsunosuka Inoue, was Japanese Ambassador in Britain from 1913-1917, his Great Grandfather Kaoru Inoue was a Koshaku (Prince) his family engaged a Jujitsu teacher at the age of nine, the teacher being Seiko Fujita who was headmaster of the Koga Ninja-Ryu. Fujita also instructed the young Inoue on Shuriken Jutsu (iron darts). When Inoue was old enough he entered university and joined the sumo club, on leaving university he started learning Karate under Master Yasuhiro Konishi, his Karate was similar to Wado-Ryu, he also learned Aikido off one of Ueshibas top students Gozo Shioda. Inoue's last art was to be his great love of his life Kobujutsu weapons his jujitsu teacher Fujita sought out the best man in Japan and may well have been the greatest weapons expert of all time Master Shinken Taira.

Taira was born in Okinawa in 1902 and learnt Kobujutsu from Master Yabuki. Inoue learned the full system, the only man to do so before Taira died in 1970 he made Inoue president of the society for the promotion of Ryu-Kyu classical martial arts started by Taira in 1935 to keep the true styles and help them survive for future generations.

The first weapon Inoue instructed his new students in was the Kon or Bo as it is usually called in the West. This is a six foot staff. Students learn the five basic blocks and attacks of the Bo followed by ten basic sparring moves with a partner. There are some twenty-two Kata for Bo, most are named after places or old master of Okinawa, such as Soeishi said to have been an expert with the Bo and born in 1680. Masters such as Sakugawa 1733-1815 left three Katas for future generations. Another great weapons master was Chatanyara, it is said he spent time in China, born in 1762 he left Sai as well as Bo Kata on the whole weapons Katas are much longer than Karate ones.

The next weapon I was instructed in was the Sai, I found that using it helped to strengthen my wrists and arms for Karate. The Sai is usually made of iron and is about 18 inches in length. Used in pairs it makes a good weapon for blocking and thrusting movements. First of all I learned the basic techniques performed on the spot. I then moved on to do nine basic fighting moves, where you are attacked by a person wielding a Bo, this was followed by the basic Kata of Sai Tsukenshitahaku. This Kata comes from a Okinawan area that was said to have many fine Sai Masters. Sai Katas can be very tiring to do. Tsukenshitahaku has 116 moves in total there are eight Kata for the Sai, out of all the weapons of Ryu-Kyu this weapon I liked the most.

My next weapon was to be the Tonfa, this weapon is said to have come from the handles of millstones used for grinding rice and made from wood. The Tonfa is spun round by the use of the handle and in practise was used in defence against the Bo. Like all the Ryu-Kyu weapons that Master Inoue teaches you first learn the basic moves so as to avoid injury before you go on to practise with a partner. The Tonfa has ten basic Kumite (fighting moves) plus two Kata, Hamahiga that is named after an Island off the coast of Okinawa and Yaraguwa Kata not too much is known about this Kata.

My next weapon was to be the one most Westerners will have seen on television or in the movies – the Nunchaku, this is two pieces of wood joined together by string or chains as many are now in the West. This weapon was said to have been used for the flailing of rice as well as the two piece there are three and four piece ones. I first learned how to swing the Nunchaku in a figure of eight swing and to the left and right using both hands. Inoue stressed that at all times great care must be taken when practising with weapons and this was very important for the Nunchaku, as at full speed it can be travelling up to 100 miles an hour from the whiplash as you swing the Nunchaku. There are three Katas for the Nunchaku which Master Inoue teaches and twelve kumite defences all against a knife using strikes to the head, body and standing leg (foreword leg) and finishing behind the attacker, for this a special Nunchaka was used made from leather and filled with cotton wool so you could make a small amount of contact to the body and legs.

The Kama (sickle) was next on the list, this weapon is used in pairs and is a very dangerous weapon to learn if not instructed correctly. First of all, Inoue teaches with wooden kamas until the students have thoroughly mastered its use, then onto the razor sharp kamas. The Katas for this weapon are Tozan and Kanigawa. Tozan Kata involves movements where you sweep the Kama near the ground as if to cut off the legs of your adversary. All the movements of the Kama Katas must be done with great care and lots of concentration, otherwise injury could be done to yourself. There are eight kumite for this weapon practised against the Bo.

My last weapon that I was to study in depth was the knuckle dusters, or Tekko, as they were known in Japan. Used in pairs the moves involved straight punches and hooks as well as practising with a partner the Kata Maizato was taught, this Kata started with a circular movement of the hands seen in the Karate Kata Ku-Shanku, this movement is also used at the start of a Sumo match and is meant to symbolize peace. Throughout my time practising Wado-Ryu and Kobudo I was struck by the similar movements of Wado-Ryu to the art Inoue taught. One evening after training I asked him if he thought the movements of present day Wado-Ryu were anything like the old styles practised in Okinawa, he said that Karate and the Ryu-Kyu martial arts were all from the same source originally and that the Katas of Wado-Ryu are nearer to the original movements of the old masters than, say, Shotokan Karate, which has changed a great deal in the last thirty years. Listening to Master Inoue I realised that he could teach me a great deal, so I decided to spend my last ten weeks training in Japan at Inoues club at Shimizu where I had all day to train and get firmly in my mind all I had learned in Japan.

Shimizu was a quite place after Tokyo and the birds could be heard singing loudly in the morning. Coming from the countryside myself I felt very much at ease away from the busy people in Tokyo. The main dojo was a superb building, it had everything a martial artist needed. Across one side of the dojo were all weapons for the use of students, it had a matted area at the end of the dojo for practising Jujitsu and Aikido techniques. I was given a small flat for my use and I rose at 4.30 each morning and started practising. I was nearly always beaten by Inoue as he used to practise from 4 – 8a.m. every day in his private dojo built onto the side of his house. His dojo was a martial artist's dream, on the wall were weapons handed down to him from past masters, some many hundreds of years old, training weights of all kinds, a skeleton that he used to practise his locks on to see how the bones worked, sand bags, all kinds of training aids and many types of Shuriken.

Shuriken jutsu is the art of throwing iron darts which also includes the star shaped weapon known in Japan as a shanken. These weapons stem from the Ninjitsu arsenal of weapons. The Ninja was a rare breed of skilled killers that were at their most lethal from around 1300 – 1600. Their main job was finding out information on enemies of their war lord. If requested they would sabotage or assassinate anything or anyone getting in the way of their lord. When shogan Tokugawa Ieyasus banned the practise of Ninjitsu in the 17th Century its practise began to decline, but still some of this art was passed down to people like Master Inoue.

Inoues school was called Shingetsu Ryu and it was with great pride that one day Inoue presented me with a book on Shuriken Jutsu written by his Instructor Seiko Fujita.

My ten weeks were passing quickly, each morning as I went to train I could hear Master Inoue practising in his dojo some times around 5 a.m., as the sun began to shine through the dojo windows. Inoue would come in and instruct me or talk about martial arts. Each Tuesday I would travel back to Tokyo in the car with Inoue where he instructed the club at the Konno shrine, these drives to and from Tokyo were fascinating as Inoue recalled old masters and talked about all kinds of martial arts. Sometimes he would go to another club at Fujinomiya, this small town is almost at the bottom of Mount Fuji.

Mr Inoue was in great demand for demonstrations but would only do a few each year. One of them he did every year was at the Meiji shrine park in Tokyo, all the top masters and their students show a little of their art to the public, I was asked to do the Tonfa Kata Hamahiga as part of the demonstration – a nice gesture to a stranger.

The Shimizu club had around 100 students, the top students being 5th Dans. They start learning weapons when they reach 1st Dan, his advanced students were instructed in the timbe, this is a shield and very often made from Turtle shell, it is used in conjunction with a rochin, a short spear that can be thrown if necessary. It has one Kata named Kanigawa. Another weapon that only advanced students are taught is the Surujin, this is a chain with a wooden handle at the end of the chain is a weight, it is used to ensnare your adversary. Master Inoue teaches a well balanced Karate similar to my style of Wado-Ryu to his advanced students, he teaches Katas of old masters not so well known in the West such as Tawata no passai, Uechi no seisan. Inoue can truly be called a Master of martial arts.

My time in Japan was coming to an end. On my last day at Shimizu I was graded second dan in Ryu-Kyu Kobudo and made a life member of the Ryu-Kyu kobudo hozon shinko kai – a nice way to end my time in Japan.

Shimizu club badge.

81

登録型名
NAME OF REGISTERED KATA
OF RYU-KYU-KOBUDO

種 （ITEMS）目	型		
BŌ 棒 術	SHŪJI 周 氏 *No.*1 小	SOEISI 添	
	〃 *No.* 2 大	〃	
	〃 OLD STYLE 古 武	SHIROTA 白	
	SAKUGAWA 佐 久 川 *No.* 1 小	〃	
	〃 *No.* 2 中	SU 末	
	〃 *No.* 3 大	S 瀬	
SAI 釵 術	TSUKENSHITAHAKU 津 堅 志 多 伯	HAN 端	
	HAMAHIGA 浜 比 嘉	湖	
	YAKĀ 屋 可 阿	TA 多	
TONFA トンファー 術	HAMAHIGA 浜 比 嘉	YA 屋	
NUNCHAKU ヌンチャク 術	*No.* 1 小 ・ *No.* 2 大	三 本 ヌ	
KAMA 二 丁 鎌 術	KANIGAWA *No.*1 *No.* 2 鐘 川 小 ・ 大	T 当	
TEKKŌ 鉄 甲 術	MAEZATO 前 里		
TINBE ティンべ 術	KANIGAWA 鐘 川		
SURUJIN スルジン 術	LONG KUSARI 長 鎖	SHOR 短	
SPECIAL BŌ 特 殊 棒 術	9 FEET BŌ 九 尺 棒	3 F 三	

82

Kind permission of M. Inoue

名 (KATA NAME)			
小 No.1	YONEKAWA 米　　川	URA SUE 浦　　添	20
大 No.2	KONGŌ 金　　剛	TSUKENSUNAKAKE 津堅砂掛	
小 No.1	TSUKENBŌ 津堅棒		
中 No.2	CHINENSHICHANAKA 知念志喜屋仲		
吉	CHATANYARA 北谷屋良		
底	CHŌUN 趙雲		
小	CHATANYARA 北谷屋良		8
城	MANGI 慈元卍		
田			2
小			3
ク			3
山			1
			1
RI 鎮			2
棒			2
		合計	42

83

History Chart

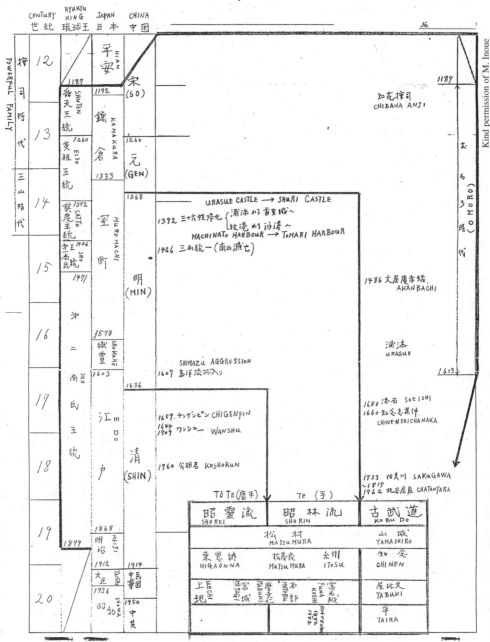

Kind permission of M. Inoue

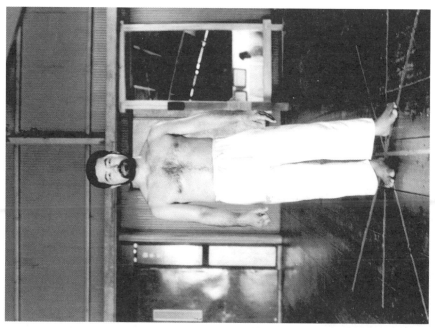

Goju-Ryu Instructor Master Higaonna

Ryu-Kyu Kobudo - Master Inoue
1918 - 1993

Frank relaxing after weapons training.

Conclusion

Since Franks return from Japan in 1979, he has continued to be active in Wado-Ryu. In 1981 he started the Budo-Arts Martial Arts Company. In 1987 Frank was the natural choice to be asked to be editor of the first major magazine on Wado-Ryu called 'Wado World', now a collectors item. In 1989 Frank was appointed to the six man committee to organise the 'World Wado Cup Championships' in London. The 1990's saw Frank direct more than twenty videos including 'The Masters' series on Wado-Ryu with Tatsuo Suzuki and Kuniaki Sakagami. Frank also commissioned 4,000 photographs for future reference on Kata Techniques.

Frank continues to teach Karate and is one of the senior instructors in the United Kingdom Karate-Do Wado-Kai. His home is in Shropshire, England.

The Secret of Karate
is
Looking for the Secret
(Master Hironori Ohtsuka 1892-1982)

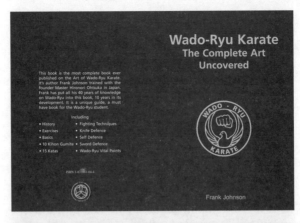
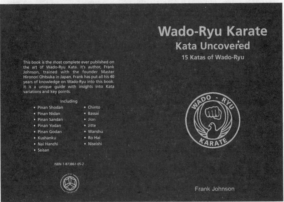
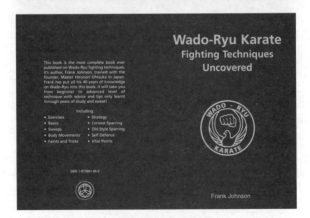